MY GURU WEARS HEELS

MY GURU WEARS HEELS

Joanna Rajendran

Waterside Productions

Printed in the United States of America

First Printing, 2021

ISBN-13: 978-1-954968-00-4 print edition
ISBN-13: 978-1-954968-01-1 ebook edition

Waterside Productions
2055 Oxford Ave
Cardiff, CA 92007
www.waterside.com

*To my muse and my maharaja, my peacock and my love ... my
Tao and my Dude.
And to everyone everywhere ... may you know that it is possible to
live your BEST. LIFE. EVER.*

TABLE OF CONTENTS

PREFACE

Did Jesus Have a Bestie?

Have you ever wondered what it feels like to be the sidekick to a larger than life world changer? Do you think Mother Teresa took breaks from comforting the needy to get an iced tea with a girlfriend? Or that maybe Gandhi sat around a fire after a particularly long march and confided in a cousin? Did Abraham Lincoln have a buddy who called him Abe and shared inside jokes?

There is nothing special about me, and yet I have had a front row seat to the awe-inspiring magic of a modern-day guru. I've witnessed so many hearts touched, so many bodies healed and so many souls renewed. I've seen people break into joyful sobs, bow to kiss her feet and wait in line to take photos. I've seen lives transformed after just one encounter.

But how? That is the question that I'm asked most often. And like many incredible endings, it didn't begin with rainbows and unicorns.

CHAPTER ONE

"From every calamity, something good will come."
—*Tao Porchon-Lynch*

I was feeling grateful for my rapist.

You did not misread that. I was seventeen years old and on summer break from the University of Albany. Seated between my mom and my sister on a boat in Italy, I felt safe for the first time in months. I had a feeling of overwhelming gratitude for the trauma from having been raped and then having had an abortion. The year was tough, and I had gotten through it on autopilot (and pot). I went to class, I did my work and I got good grades. But I also felt broken and out of control. I felt stupid that I had put myself in danger. The rapist was a guy I was dating casually. He was enlisting in the Marines and I told him from the beginning that our relationship wouldn't be a sexual one. That seemed to be fine for him—until it wasn't. The night before he enlisted, he came to my house and together we went to a hotel in New Jersey.

It was supposed to be a big send-off for him with lots of people, but instead it turned out to be just the two of us in a room. Before that, I had always thought that I could handle myself; that I was street smart (or as street smart as a girl could be growing up in Westchester County). I can still see his dark eyes distorted with anger as he pinned me down. His smile from earlier in the day had vanished and he grit his teeth as saliva pooled in the corners of his mouth. I didn't recognize the man on top me. He looked more like a rabid dog. I once read that in moments of intense fear, people dissociate to survive. I think that's bullshit as I felt the exact opposite. My senses were heightened. I smelled his salty sweat, I tasted stale beer from his angry mouth, and I was pissed off that the summer's strength-training workouts I had been doing weren't enough to muscle him to GET THE FUCK OFF ME. As tears fell

1

down my face, I tried biting him and wiggling away. Ultimately, all I could really do was wish for the end to come quickly.

But the true shame I felt had layers to it. When I got home the next day, I was sad and scared and humiliated. When I found out that my mother's jewelry was missing, I was furious. The day before, I had thought nothing of having this guy in my house. He had been there before. So, as I was showering and throwing some things in a bag for our night out, I didn't wonder about what he might be up to. I didn't have any reason to believe that he would go into my mother's room or more specifically, into her jewelry box. But when my mom, who we called Bo, asked if anyone had been in the house and then showed me the empty spaces in her Oriental jewelry cabinet, I felt like I had been kicked in the stomach. A stomach that was already churning and eating itself from the trauma of the night before.

The pieces were symbols of my naïveté, sentiments of my mom's heart, both of which had been robbed. The one man who had fallen in love with Bo, after she and my dad split, proposed to her. He'd given her a gold ring and it was all that she had left when he tragically died shortly thereafter. The ring was gone! I wanted to throw up. I had gotten out of the car in my driveway only minutes before, and all I could think of was relief that I would never have to see the rapist again. But seeing the jewelry box shifted my feelings to pure anger. My poor taste in men had left my mom vulnerable. Anger and vomit overcame me, and I ran to the bathroom.

Even with the traumatic events in life, if you change one thing, you change everything. And in this case, the shattered confidence and the stolen jewelry led me to an entirely new path. My mom used the insurance money to take my sister and me on our first international trip to Italy. She couldn't take seeing her strong-willed daughter be reduced to sweating and sobbing in her father's old bathrobe—a worn piece of blue terrycloth with *ALAN* written in script across the chest. I remember lying on the fluffy grey living room carpet thinking this is what people mean when they say "breakdown." I don't think my mother knew what to do but she was smart enough to think that if I was officially losing it, then losing it in Italy would be a nicer option.

So here we were in Venice. On this particular day, as we floated in a gondola moving across the water, I looked up at the clouds and saw them. FELT THEM, for the first time. Suddenly they were more vast and majestic than I had ever noticed. More than that, I felt that I was the cloud ... and the water ... and all of it. Something shifted. Something opened. I felt connected. I was as connected in that very moment as I had been disconnected in all the moments leading up to it. There was a knowing and a peace that came from this knowing. My fear evaporated in an instant and the feeling that I was a part of it all was intoxicating. The same magic that created the world, that formed those clouds and that water, was inside of me and I experienced an all-consuming sense of lightness and wonder. It was like being high but better because this version came with utter clarity.

The new lightness of being that began in Venice started showing up in other parts of my life. I was feeling more open to the notion of following this spiritual path to see where it led. Though when it came to trying yoga, it was way less obvious (and a bit more superficial) than that. I had browsed an article while getting my nails done about Madonna sharing that her lean, strong muscles and peace of mind were the result of switching her fitness routine exclusively to yoga. We had done a lot of walking and sightseeing in Italy, and a LOT of eating, so my body was definitely not in Madonna-shape. But Italian men apparently love voluptuousness and the longer we were there, the more whistles I seemed to attract. Though once back on American soil, I was going to the gym and taking classes daily and after a typical body sculpting class with weights, I saw that the class the following day in the same time slot was yoga. I decided to try it. Little did I know it would change my life.

The next morning I arrived at 9:30. As I entered, an older woman at the front of the room sat waiting in what I would come to learn was called full lotus with her long legs folded on top of each other like a pretzel. She was dressed in a form-fitting bodysuit and leggings. She wore big earrings and a large pendant necklace. Her lips were made bold with pinkish red lipstick. My assessment (aka judgement) didn't stop there. For a woman with a short torso, her legs did seem impossibly long. And her face, although lined with age, was still stunning. When I realized that her silver and black hair was likely a wig, I wondered how she would be able to teach yoga while keeping it in place. Then a moment later I was completely skeptical that this cute older woman in this tiny little package could give me the Madonna butt kicking I thought I had signed up for. She glanced up at the door and then her eyes landed on mine. I was drawn in. Immediately. Completely. Like villages to a river or a cold traveler to a fire. She was light. She was healing. She was magic. It was an energy that radiated from her—an aura that surrounded her and when our eyes connected, I felt a surge of that energy; of love. I can only explain it as goose bumps and tingles on the inside instead of on the surface of my skin. Never a religious person, this was the first time I understood truly what devout people feel in the spiritual presence of their deity.

I sat directly in front of her and immediately took the same pose. Though brand new to yoga, I was naturally flexible and felt proud that I could do with my legs what she was doing with hers. Cocky, I started thinking what any arrogant young New Yorker would: *I'm rocking yoga!* And that was when I really met Tao Porchon-Lynch. In her 70s, it would be years until she was acknowledged as a master teacher and the world's oldest yoga teacher by *The Guinness Book of Records*. It would be decades until the world caught wind of what those lucky enough to be in her direct vicinity already knew. She was the real deal and she was right in front of me. Unfolding from her yogic pose, she stood and approached. Tiny, she seemed to float rather than walk. Her toothpick-like legs were almost her whole length. She was elegant and adorable all at once. The first thing that struck me in this close proximity was the twinkle in her impossibly blue sparkly eyes. The first words she spoke to me were, "That's very nice. But it isn't yoga."

I was baffled, and it must have shown. I had been so smug about what I thought was my first – ever yoga pose in her class that looked exactly like hers. I wondered what she could possibly mean by that comment.

She continued, "Let me guess. You probably have always been able to do that, yes?"

"Yes."

Throughout the class, Tao taught alignment cues and guided us into different poses. She would demonstrate how one small adjustment with the foot would energize the entire leg or free the hip. Her tips seemed so simple, but those slight movements would create space for the breath to flow. Her teaching made everything possible. My body began to dance through the poses. I felt graceful and strong. The first time I was in a forward fold, I was surprised that my hands didn't reach the floor. Considering I had already anointed myself a yoga expert in the first minute of class, this lack of range came as a shock. But by the second forward fold, my fingertips were tickling the mat. She had gotten me to use my breath so effectively that I was seeing a difference in my range of motion, and by the last forward fold, I had full palms flat on the ground. And I got it! Truly got it. Yoga wasn't about coming already done. It was about the unfolding. Finding space. Space in your body. Space in your breath. Space between thoughts. Happiness through the tears that fall from your eyes.

I began to practice regularly with Tao and after some time, yoga would extend to a tea or light meal afterward. Since she hardly seemed to eat or need normal mortal sustenance at all, we had a lot of time to connect. In fact, she had already explained in class one day that she never drank water. When I commented on how little food she ate, she explained that there is more energy to be consumed in the air than people realize and that they too could experience it if they learned to breathe properly.

It was during a lunch at an outdoor café that I asked her what I had thought would be a simple question that would have a fittingly simple answer. But instead, my asking where Tao was born would lead to my first dive into the magical story that is her life.

"I was born on a ship. And since I'm rather impatient when I want to do something, I came two months early."

It was 1918 and the ship that sailed from Europe to Canada transported Tao's father and his pregnant wife. During the journey her mother went into labor prematurely, and as Tao took her first breath, her mother took her last. When she told me that, I got chills everywhere. I couldn't even imagine being born and then never knowing the touch, feel and love of your own mom.

Tao's father had no way of caring for baby Tao so it was decided that she would go to India to be raised by her uncle. All of this, what would determine her entire life's path, was decided so quickly. What seemed like an unspeakably tragic start to her life is what Tao came to consider an auspicious beginning.

"I'm very blessed, you know? Because I never knew my mother and I only saw my father once, but if it didn't unfold the way it did, I wouldn't have been raised by my uncle. If you look for the good, Dear, you'll always find it."

Her uncle, or "Oncle," as she called him, was an incredible man. He was smart and kind and curious and spiritual. His work took him all over and he brought young Tao with him on his travels. He fostered Tao's natural sense of wonder and became her first true teacher. For instance, one day, when she was just a girl, her aunt caught Tao with her head on the ground. When she asked what she was up to, much to her chagrin, Tao answered that she was listening to the grass grow. Her aunt complained to Oncle that she was "off." But he understood, and he continued to understand and to encourage her unquenchable thirst for knowledge.

Oncle also taught her to respect all people and to know that everyone was her equal. When they encountered a farmer who couldn't read, he shared with her a lesson that would stay with Tao always.

"You are no higher than that man, Tao. There is no one who is beneath you. Just because he cannot read does not make him illiterate. For he is a farmer and he knows more about the soil than you or I ever could. There is something we can learn from everyone and everything."

Oncle was well regarded in the community and people sought his company. One day, Tao returned home to find a small in stature man with round glass sitting with him. That was the first time that she met Gandhi—there, in the living room of their home. People were streaming in to meet this humbly dressed man and young Tao was intrigued. Later, Oncle would tell her to pack some things—"not many and nothing fancy"—in a bag. Accustomed to such adventure, she did so without question. Little did Tao know that she was packing to join with Gandhi in the famous Salt Marches.

The Salt March was something that would shift Tao in perpetuity. Being with Oncle, she was used to living in his teachings that all were united and that everything was possible. But now for the first time, she was seeing violence, prejudice and cruelty. The British soldiers would beat the peaceful protesters. Tao was shocked to see that the people, unless crying in pain, did not resist nor retaliate. She held tightly onto Oncle's hand.

Even in the midst of her first exposure to violence, Tao took in the beautiful people and the beautiful country. For she knew—even at the age of 11—that it wasn't what you saw that counted, it was what you noticed. She chose to notice all the people together in oneness for a purpose in which they believed. She became present to the power of peace and witnessed, firsthand, what was possible when you combated violence with peace, injustice with dignity and hate with love.

CHAPTER TWO

"Lead us from the unreal into the real;
from darkness into the light of inner knowledge."
—*Tao Porchon-Lynch*

Renee Diamond was a goddess. A former dancer and bodybuilder, she used her form like an artist would a brush. She too was drawn to Tao's light. When they met, Renee says she was a "beaten up, broken down aerobics teacher in desperate need of help." Under Tao's guidance, Renee transformed her teachings into a more complete, spiritual use of mind and body. I loved them both completely. And even though I had taken Renee's fitness classes for years, this new common thread of yoga in general, and in following Tao specifically, began to bond us in a completely new way.

Renee had blonde hair that was always expertly and stylishly cut. She made complete eye contact—her ocean-blue eyes seemed to bore into you as she spoke—and held it, something far too rare. For all the grace and glam that Tao brought to her classes, Renee brought a "badassness" that was intoxicating. Her muscles had muscles and yet she managed to maintain a feminine softness too. When practicing with her, I felt so fluid as if I was moving through honey. With Tao, I did yoga like a ballroom dancer. With Renee, more like a primitive; a tribeswoman. If Tao's classes were like gliding through a tango, Renee's were like grinding to reggae. Different and the same. Simple and powerful. My practice was evolving, and I was ready. I was seeking.

Some people enter your life quietly and leave just the same. Others come in with a fire and leave you with nothing but smoke. At this point in my life, I was reeling in a moment of change. Actually, two moments. Two changes. Two losses.

7

My yoga practice had helped me to heal, to find peace, to move beyond. I graduated from college and changed directions completely. I had always planned to go to law school and become a lawyer like my dad. And then the summer of yoga happened. One day after class Tao told me about her many incarnations, personally and professionally. Something that she said stayed with me then and continues to. She said when an opportunity presented itself to do it and to do it right away. And since there are no coincidences, during the same time period I was given a gorgeous book as a gift. Kevyn Aucoin, a talented makeup artist, had a book of incredible transformations. He used makeup to change famous actors and models into completely different characters, genders and ethnicities. The book was mesmerizing, and helped me realize that I could take a hobby and turn it into a career. I called home to tell my dad that I wouldn't be going to law school. I had geared myself up for what I was sure would be a serious and long discussion. But I should have known better. My dad is like Atticus Finch. And like the well-known father in *To Kill A Mockingbird*, he is honest, strong and unfailingly fair.

"Dad"

"Josie"

"I don't think I'm going to go to law school."

"I know."

"What do you mean you know? I just decided today." This was not at all the way the conversation that I had rehearsed in my head over and over again was supposed to go.

"Josie, I've been waiting for this call for three years. You're a creative person. Do something creative and enjoy your life."

I was absolutely stunned. He and I had discussed my legal career since the days of watching *L.A. Law* together on the living room floor of the apartment he bought after splitting from my mom.

"Hello? Jo?"

"I'm here. I'm surprised. You always told me I'd make such a great lawyer."

"And you would. But you wouldn't be a happy one. You say you like criminal law but you'd be with people in the most miserable times of their lives."

I paused. Digesting this suddenly felt like my dad had been the one to have the epiphany and that I'd just gotten the memo.

"Okay. Thanks Dad. And in that case, I think I want to be a makeup artist."

"Yup. Sounds about right."

And just like that, instead of thinking about applications for law school, I was boarding a plane for London where I would do my last semester of college abroad and fall for Antonio, an Italian man with questionable morals. Surprisingly, that relationship lasted longer than my eight months in Europe and we spent the next three years bouncing between America, Italy and England. It was incredible. We traveled the world. I learned Italian. He taught me how to drive on either side of the car and either side of the road and every possible combination of the two. He was my first boyfriend to wear tight jeans, to have a mortgage and to buy me plane tickets. On one flight while traveling to visit him, I even had a flight attendant bring me into the cockpit for a champagne toast for no reason at all. Chatting in both English and Italian with the crew, mid-flight as they smoked cigarettes; such were the adventures in a pre-9/11 time of international travel.

Being a makeup artist proved to be a career flexible enough to go along with this phase of my life. I was building my portfolio and experiencing the world. And like most phases, this, and Antonio, had a shelf life.

I remember the exact moment that I met Antonio in the first week of my London life. I had walked into a crowded London nightclub with a new girlfriend. We were making our way through the bar looking for a place to sit, when I feel a touch on my elbow and looked down to see a man sitting with gelled jet-black hair and a flirty grin.

"Tell me something. Where are you going?" His accent was thick. And sexy.

"To find a place to sit." I was guarded, very New Yorkish. I had been this way since the rape. I could have fun, but it still felt weird to flirt and to be flirted with.

"You can sit on my lap." But he said it like "seet on my lop."

My walls started crumbling. "I don't know you. I'm not going to sit on your lap."

Clearly, he didn't know that New York girls didn't fall for such bullshit. "Antonio." He shook my hand. "Nice to meet you. Now you can sit on my lap."

Walls gone.

He didn't get me to sit on his lap, but he did make me laugh. And that got me to sit down next to him on the seat where his friend was before he kicked him out of it. A few minutes into our chat, I noticed a large and shiny watch on his wrist. When I complimented him on it, his admission drew me in further.

"May I be honest with you? It isn't working at the moment. I only wear it to be fashionable." I loved the confidence of his overall image and the humor and the vulnerability of admitting to wearing the broken watch. He gave me my first night tour of London and after driving over Tower Bridge, he, his friend, my friend and I stopped at a café for an espresso. But it was when I proceeded to order a hot chocolate instead, that he became smitten.

For the following years, we typically spent summers and Christmases in Italy, and once a month, one of us would visit the other for a brief stay. This arrangement kept us together longer than we would have lasted if we were in the same country. It's easier to think fondly of a person when writing romantic letters than it is to live with them and watch them pick their nose. And their ass. It turned out this Italian always seemed to have his hand down the back of his pants. Maybe it was the tight jeans?

After about three years, the novelty was wearing off. He was due to visit me and celebrate my sister's bridal shower. When he got off the plane, his first comment removed any lingering doubt as to whether the relationship had run its course. It had been about six weeks since we had last seen each other—the longest stretch to date. I committed to giving it one last real effort and had spent the day having my nails done, straightening my long hair and putting on an outfit chic enough for a European's taste and matching it with oversized sunglasses. (For Italians, without a stylish watch and a nice pair of sunglasses you may as well be naked. The watch, a Cartier he had given me the previous Christmas in a room full of old "connected" men in cardigans; the sunglasses, he had carefully selected in the small village shop owned by his cousin. At 5'8" I am pretty tall and I enhanced my look with long black pants and trendy boots that had a heel. My dark brown hair looked shiny and straight thanks to the effort I had put in earlier. Before leaving the car, I assessed my makeup in the rearview mirror. The makeup always had to be thoughtfully applied when it came to Antonio. He liked a bit of smoky shadow as long as it was done sub-tly and well blended. Usually I used bronzer instead of blush so I could have a "glowy" finish. I don't really resemble anyone in my family and have often thought (or have been told) that I look Native American. With my training in makeup and playing with highlights and shadows, I learned to exaggerate already high cheekbones and to make brown eyes look more dimensional. I also knew to forego lips altogether or to go for a clear gloss. This behavior of adapting who I was and how I was dressing, speaking and being had shifted in small ways over time. It was so gradual that I hardly realized that even while wearing shoes that made me look taller, I was making myself smaller.

Satisfied with my reflection, I adjusted my bra making sure that I was showing the carefully chosen amount of cleavage. My boobs came when I was around 13 and have been getting in the way ever since. Naturally busty, I was totally comfortable wearing outfits that highlighted them. Antonio less so. If I was showing too much for his liking, he would say something like "close the ween-doe." Boobs showing just a hint of cleavage in my long-sleeved V-neck shirt, I jumped out of the car and walked to the terminal.

Usually when I'd spot him in his way-too-tight black jeans, way-too-gelled hair and way-too-exaggerated strut, I'd have a feeling of anticipation. But the butterflies that had become part of the airport pickup ritual had clearly reverted to caterpillars. This time, he approached and instead of the typical greeting of a kiss and an appreciative glance, he simply looked me up and down and scowled.

"Tell me something ... what are you wearing?"

Suddenly years of adapting to a worldly lifestyle and doing my best to tame such "American" habits like cursing and being independent became more than I could bear.

"Fuck you."

And such began the silent ride back to my father's apartment. We had an uneventful night together devoid of a date or even food. Antonio claimed to be tired and went to bed without saying anything.

The next morning, I woke up and got dressed and ready to make the day as special as possible for my sister. Jen was two years older, smart, kind, funny and loyal. She was my best friend and I would do anything in the world for her. This was her day. And so, I ignored the fact that Antonio was moping as I was primping. I ignored that he had yet to touch me. I ignored the fact that I left the house in a tight black dress with makeup selected to be pretty and still daytime appropriate, all without a comment from him. Basically, I ignored him altogether. I planned to be fully present for Jen and to be the best maid of honor for her bridal shower. After, I would come home and have a "talk" with the Italian.

But there would be no "after."

The plan was that my dad would come to the end of the shower with my brother, soon-to-be brother-in-law, and Antonio. They would do the obligatory schmoozing and then help pack up all the gifts. Only there was no Antonio.

"Where is he?"

"Dunno. I went by the apartment and he wasn't there." My dad looked like the bearer of bad news.

"Did he say where he was going?"

"I never spoke to him. I went for a haircut and when I got back, he wasn't there." The man never uses extra words. He's more like the old detectives on the show *Dragnet*: "Just the facts, ma'am."

And I knew. I knew in my heart what the note would later confirm. You hear stories, at least in country songs, about a man going out for cigarettes and never coming back. Some people skip town when the shit hits the fan. Apparently, my man skipped country.

The relationship that was the bridge between my adolescent and adult life had ended and I would never see him again.

Right around then, my grandmother, my Mommom, was starting to become ill. Until meeting Tao, Mommom was the only person who looked at me with love-filled translucent-blue eyes. She was tall and had a presence of confidence. She was strong and bold in her beliefs and convictions. She saw me as a young girl trying to hide what I thought was my chubby adolescent body as I got out of her Florida pool and made my future confidence her personal mission. She would tell me how important it was that tall girls never give away their confidence by shrinking. She said how I "carried myself" would make people in life respect what I had to say. This was hard to grasp when at a sixth grade dance, the boys came up to my belly button.

Throughout my life, she was a harbor. When our parents divorced, Mommom and Poppop were there to be the calm in the storm, the peace in the transition. Though she was my father's mother, she remained close to my mom for the rest of her life. Most people have a grandmother, I had a Mommom.

It was a blessing I recognized at the time and not just nostalgically after the fact. She used to say that "no one had what we had," referring to the closeness our fractured family maintained. She played practical jokes on us, attended every milestone and listened to anything we had to say.

Mommom was horrified that my mom's idea of a vegetable was a side salad, that my brother liked ravioli in a can, that we didn't know how to sew and that I wore big hoop earrings with my name ornamentally engraved in them. And yet, she understood each of us as her uniquely different kids. She called my sister Jen her Curly Girly, my brother Jonny her Special and I was Cookie. She would laugh at our inside jokes and say that we were "jerky kids." Mommom recognized that I was different and would often say to my mom, "I don't know where we got this one. She's not like anyone else but we'll keep her."

Then one day she was diagnosed with cancer and given a short time. If something didn't meet Mommom's standards, it simply wouldn't do. Cancer was no exception. She had just leased a new car, was still working in my father's law office, wanted to see my sister get married and my brother graduate college. This diagnosis didn't work with her plan.

Clearly, she made an arrangement with some kind of higher power. For Mommom had taught me how to make her matzoh balls and how to dress properly for temple. But she also had taught me that you didn't need to go to a certain building to pray or to a cemetery to think of a loved one. Like Tao, she was instrumental in teaching me that that feeling came from within. When Poppop passed away, ever the pillar of strength and dignity, rather than to personally mourn the loss of her husband of over fifty years, she instead was instantly concerned with protecting the "kids." The thought of missing our milestones wouldn't cut it, and her insistence that she never would was heard by us all.

The diagnosis turned out to be miraculously less severe, or at least, staved off until she completed what she needed to complete in this lifetime. She was radiant at Jen's wedding, glowing with pride and joy. By the time it came to go to my brother's graduation, her illness had returned but it wouldn't deter her. She took a cane... I say "took" because instead of using it, she would walk carrying it! Such is the way of a strong, stubborn woman. When we were seated in the ceremony, I worried about her newly frail demeanor and kept asking if she was okay.

"I'm more than okay. I'm seeing my special graduate."

"It's a really long ceremony Mommom. Do you want to leave in a bit and go to the hotel and rest?"

"No."

"Are you sure? We have the dinner tonight. It might be a lot."

"I want to see them throw the hats."

I knew better than to argue. The ceremony itself was painfully dull but seeing the pleasure on Mommom's face was something that would stay with me always.

After what seemed like seven hours, the graduation was coming to an end. And as they congratulated the class of 2002, one single hat flew into the air. Apparently, they had warned the students that the traditional hat toss was dangerous and that they were not to do it under any circumstances. Out of the thousands of students, only one graduate disobeyed. It was my brother.

He had no way of knowing what Mommom was saying to me in the audience, but such was their connection that it didn't surprise me it was his hat we saw take flight.

One month later Mommom was gone.

And our ladybug took her place. In the years to come, she would still be at every milestone. At every death, birth, highlight and defeat. Whenever we needed her, we would see a ladybug. This was so undeniable that even the "normal" people in our family believed it. Like as soon as my sister found out that she had lost a baby far into her pregnancy, a yellow ladybug landed on her belly and stayed there.

On what would've been her due date for that baby, Jen came with me to assist Tao as she led a workshop at the yoga center Kripalu. After teaching her last class of the weekend, we celebrated in Tao's private room with a glass of wine from the bottle that we had snuck in. Tao sat on the bed, while the desk lamp on the nearby table created a halo of light on the wall behind her. My sister, another assistant and I sat on the floor gazing up at her and chatting. Jen, the quieter sister, asked me to ask Tao if she would be able to have another baby. Wanting so badly to believe but still so raw from her loss, she was reluctant to hear the answer. Tao answered emphatically, "Yes. Of course. Of course you'll have another baby! And he's coming soon."

As the words came out of her mouth, a ladybug appeared within the halo of light on the wall. Inside. In the winter. In the mountains of the Berkshires.

It was a powerful reminder that love is energy and it can never die. We kept Mommom's energy alive by talking about her and she let us feel her's by transitioning from our "Perpetual Lady" to our "Ladybug."

The following month Jen found out she was pregnant with a boy.

After Mommom died, I was even more grateful for the special connection that Tao and I had forged. She told me that the first time she ever saw me, she knew we were meant to be together and to do great things. "There's something in you that's special and when you enter a room, you make people feel happy." I was so humbled to hear her speak of me in the way that I and so many others thought of her to be. She continued, "Many people come to my classes and do beautiful yoga. But not all of them live their practice. You do. You have eyes that twinkle like a little girl's. They are filled with wonder. And love. And you share the love in a way that isn't put on. It's your soul. Just look how much time you spend putting up with me."

The more I was with Tao, the more I realized that she had an incredible sense of humor to go along with her wisdom. Often while teaching, she would say something so deep and yet incredibly simple. Then, she would follow it with something so witty and genuinely funny. In these intimate conversations, I came to realize that it wasn't just wisdom and humor but the fact that it was matched with unbelievable humility that took my breath away. She truly didn't realize what a marvel she was. She assumed that all beings were miracles and treated each as such. When people would flock to her workshops to soak up every morsel of her teaching, she would say things like, "I just hope I haven't bored you." That sentence, when you think about all she had to teach and to offer, is mind blowing. The closer we became, the more intimately she would share about her past.

It was World War II and Tao was in England. She had emigrated from India by way of France and nothing about the journey was simple.

She left her beloved country in the hopes of reconnecting with her father who was serving with the French Canadians in the war. Upon arriving in France, Tao connected with an aunt who owned and operated a vineyard. Though the property was not yet in the part of France that was occupied, the Germans were beginning to make their presence known.

As a young woman, Tao began noticing people working on the property who looked different from her. When her curiosity was piqued enough to inquire, her aunt would quickly divert the subject. In an effort to protect Tao, her aunt pretended that her work and travels were just vineyard business as usual. But as time went on, Tao would learn that her aunt was actively helping to hide Jewish families and to arrange their safe passage out of France. Tao wanted to help. Concerned about putting her in danger, her aunt would use Tao only as necessary; mostly to go to stores and pass or receive messages or to go to the convent to secure Catholic garb for nuns and priests for the Jewish families to wear as disguises while they traveled to escape the Nazis.

Like Gandhi, Tao's aunt became another source of inspiration to others. They saw injustice and took action. They did what they could with what they had. Tao's aunt actually rigged the large vats in her vineyard to still function even while emptied. When German soldiers came to the property, she would offer them a glass of wine and pour it from the cleverly altered vats leaving them none the wiser that entire families were hidden in silence within. When Tao would ask why she was helping so many people she didn't even know, her aunt replied that she would do the same if she did know them. When Tao went on to ask if she was scared, her aunt said that no one would suspect an "old woman" to be anything other than as she appeared.

When France fell to the Nazis, her aunt insisted that Tao leave for England while she could. It was a phase of Tao's life that included beautiful hellos and far too many goodbyes.

Despite being exposed to typhoid, dangerous encounters with soldiers and suspicious customs officers (they didn't quite know what to make of an Indian woman in a sari with a French passport), Tao made it to England.

With no money, no accommodations and very little grasp of the English language, this new beginning required courage and more than a bit of divine intervention. She would check daily with the embassy to inquire about her father. After a few months, she got word that he would be leaving with his battalion by train, but that if she hurried, she could meet him. The woman who gave her the news escorted Tao and they made it to the crowded platform as the train was being boarded. It was there that Tao was introduced to her father for the first time. She searched his face, desperately trying to commit every feature to memory as he did hers. Within moments, the last call to board was announced and he was gone. That was the only time she would meet him.

Throughout all the change, all the travel and all the uncertainty, Tao was never afraid. She expected something good to come along and it always did.

Wondering where she would go and to whom she would turn, she met a woman who recognized her from a hotel in India where Tao had visited with her Oncle. Surah remembered Tao for her beautiful Indian dancing and her elegant hand movements. This friend soon after introduced her to a night-club owner who spoke French. And so began Tao's career as a dance host in England.

Dancing with different men through a language barrier was proving more difficult and Tao felt more vulnerable than she had thought she would. Made to wear very revealing outfits, being so close to the men made her uncomfortable. The circumstances of life, however, were so trying at the time that she knew better than to complain. There were bombings every night. As Tao was working, people were taking to the Underground for refuge. Refusing to allow fear to overtake her, she would walk through the bombings to get to the nightclub. After a brief (and failed attempt) at blending in as a chorus girl, she teamed up with some other women and went on to create her own cabaret show. She much preferred to be dancing on the stage for the crowd rather than with the men comprising it. It wasn't long before she developed a reputation for being fearless and a true following of grateful fans ensued, including an American journalist in England reporting on the nightly bombings.

His pieces were titled "Darkest London," but when he began to follow Tao and saw the impact she had in those frightening times, he wrote that he must change the name to "Brighter London." At this point Tao was dancing in five of the most well-known clubs in central London, performing for the wealthy and famous and would walk from place to place in the time of night when most were hiding. When asked if she ever felt afraid, her answer was always a simple "no."

This was one of many aspects about her that surprised me. Generations apart in age, yet Tao and I shared so much in common. As she told stories of her cabaret days, I would share similar ones with her. Since connecting with Tao (and disconnecting from Antonio) I had moved out of my father's apartment and into the first place that I bought on my own. I was also supplementing my makeup income by working as a cocktail waitress. One reason was because the money was so good, but another was because it was a way to rebel against the stifling energy that I felt from years of trying to be an American version of a good Italian girlfriend. Antonio would despise the thought of me working in a nightclub, dressed in almost nothing and being the subject of attention of strange men. But he no longer had a say and I was taking full advantage. I was reclaiming my independence and sexual power. I started with regular clubs and moved up to being a waitress in their VIP rooms. But the last club that I would work at was a bit different.

I was in the champagne room of a very exclusive "gentlemen's" club in New York City surrounded by two professional athletes, six "entertainers" and champagne that cost more than my mortgage.

I was doing makeup professionally and yoga casually. Having taken Tao's classes for years now, I felt confident that I could bring my light wherever I went. But that was more challenging every Tuesday and Thursday night when I was a cocktail waitress in a very expensive strip club. Everything was an illusion. The customers exchanged dollars for club currency we called "funny money" and proceeded to use it to pay women to distract them for an hour in a room the size of a closet. They would pay the doorman to enter, the host to seat them, another host to bring them a woman, the woman to dance, the host to book a private room and the security guy to keep it private, the waitress for the champagne, the waiter for the food, the bathroom attendant, the masseuse, the valet. It was a world in which everything had a price and everything was for sale.

As waitresses, our uniforms were black and sexy; the skimpier the better. After three years working two nights a week, I had perfected my most profitable look. A tight black blazer with a bra underneath that showed ample cleavage and a vinyl mini skirt that showed more than ample leg. The heels had laces that wrapped around my ankles and looked sexy, but were actually quite functional for running up and down stairs with trays of cocktails. I wore my long brown hair slicked back in a braided ponytail. The final touch was that same pair of glasses Antonio had chosen for me in the village shop. I remember asking him why he was looking at nonprescription glasses for me since he already knew I had perfect vision, and his answer was simple: "These are for the sex, Banana."

Years later and for a whole new audience, his words proved prophetic. In a place where sex was so obviously on display, the comparatively demure look of being a "good girl in a bad place" was very effective.

On a particularly memorable night, we had a famous actor in one of the private rooms, two actresses in the restaurant section, a well-known pop singer in another room and a handsome but short Italian businessman in another. When I entered the room to bring the businessman a fifth bottle of champagne, I realized in that moment that I had almost become immune to what I was seeing. Lorenzo was perfectly dressed. His grey suit was expertly tailored. His hair precisely cut. His nails beautifully manicured. Had he grown about six more inches, he would have been close to perfection; a gorgeous mix of George Clooney and Bradley Cooper. But he hadn't, and that left me wondering if it had something to do with his need to be surrounded by ten topless dancers. Ten different women, all beautiful. Twenty breasts on display. Lorenzo was in the center of all with stacks of "funny money" on the table before him. As I poured the champagne, he spoke to me in heavily accented English.

"Can you stay and have a drink with us?"

"I have other rooms. But I can quickly toast with you." This was something we often did to ensure that the guests were having fun and that their bottles went dry more quickly.

"Bravo."

I poured. We toasted. We sipped. The dancers giggled and gossiped. Flirted and teased. A few began dancing. Lorenzo and I started talking about Italy and he was excited when I said *"auguri"* instead of "cheers."

"Perche parle Italiano?"

"Perche avevo un ragazzo Italiano."

Even in the midst of chaos, it was possible at times for me to find spots of normalcy ... until something jarred me back to what it really was. As he and I were speaking, one dancer came and sat on his lap. Another began caressing his ear. On the sofa next to us, two girls were giving lap dances to two others. But he kept his eyes on me.

"So, what would it take for you to get undressed?"

"There's nothing."

"Come on, Bella. Everyone has a price."

"No thank you. But luckily you have all the naked beauty you could want already in this room." Usually that was enough to deflect the attention back to the dancers and sneak away from the extra grabby, extra pervy customers.

"You see that table?" He was gesturing toward the one with stacks of "funny money" on it.

"Yes."

"If you show me your tits once, you can have it all."

Well-dressed does not always mean well-mannered.

I glanced at the table. I was guessing there had to be at least $5,000 in the pile. As if reading my thoughts, Lorenzo continued, "That's $10,000. If you show me those tits, the ones that aren't for sale, it's yours."

This is the part of the story where almost every single person I have since told, has said, "I would've done it." Even my own father said it. Though I'm sure he only said it because I didn't.

It was one of those moments where I felt myself standing at a crossroad. To date, I had managed to maintain my spirituality in a strip club. In fact, I had made a practice of going on yoga retreats at least every six months to undo some of what I was experiencing in that environment. My trips to Kripalu were therapeutic. But that night, with Lorenzo, it became clear that everyone had a line, a moral guidepost and I had securely found mine. I had an apartment that I had proudly bought myself. I had an incredible family. I knew that if I really needed $10,000, I had choices. Looking around at the "entertainers," some of them having come from similarly amazing families as mine, and yet their one choice led to another until taking their clothes off for money became a thing that was possible. I never wanted that to be something that was possible for me. I settled for a decent tip and snuck out of Lorenzo's room. The minute I left I realized that while this had been a lightbulb moment of clarity and a check of my moral fiber, for Lorenzo I was already a forgotten blip on the screen of his night.

Our choices are snowballs that gain avalanche-like momentum. We are in complete control as to whether those snowballs are collecting more of the positive or more of the negative.

I would think back to the stories that Tao would tell me. She too had this "nightlife" aspect to her life in addition to acting and modeling. I was so taken by the fact that regardless of where she was in the world or with whom, she had always been able to maintain her sense of self. Even with famous actors and writers and powerful men, most of whom had eyes for her. She seemed to have handled it all in stride with so much grace.

During my time waitressing, but for an occasional dalliance with a semi-famous actor, I would spend my nightlife surrounded by sex and then my nights in bed alone. I had an occasional time filler but no one taking up space in my heart. One night while at work, I checked my cell phone that I kept in a glass by the register. I saw a simple text:

In town. Meet me at the Waldorf when ur done.

I briefly debated whether I wanted to go to the famous hotel when my shift ended at two a.m. The deliberation had less to do with the late hour than the fact that I wasn't wearing a "good" bra and underwear combination. Every girl can relate to the difference between the set you wear when there's a chance someone might see it to those you wear when you know they won't. I also had a bit of stubble on my leg. Besides, after another night of having sweaty people touch me, flirt with me and a few spill drinks on me, I wasn't sure I was in the mood. He must have sensed this:

Don't think. Just come.

Fine.

The club's bouncer walked me to my car. This was a ritual we repeated every night I worked and one I promised my parents that I would never overlook. As we waited for my car to be pulled up by the valet, I remembered the emergency razor that I'd taken from the gym and stashed in the center console.

Then, stopped at a red light, two guys in the car next to me signaled for me to roll down my window. I obliged and as they asked where the party was and if I wanted to help them find it, I laughed at the thought that as they attempted to flirt, I was doing a dry shave of my legs. Single life in the single years. Almost to the hotel, I began talking to the "parking angels" as I looked for a spot. I had learned that the process to get anything you wanted in life was actually very simple and I loved to use parking spaces in NYC as practice. It did not fail.

As I thanked the parking angels and hid the razor back in the center console, I checked the mirror only to see that I still looked like the night I just had. And even though I kept the windows down for much of the ride, I was sure I still smelled like it too. It was a specific combination of lime, sex, perfume and smoke.

Walking across the famous lobby to the elevator, I wondered *what exactly am I doing here?* Again. What was the pull? And then, as usual, I remembered. In high school, my girlfriends and I used to sit around the basement of one friend's house and watch the same movie over and over again. It was about a singing group, and typical of young girls, we each had our favorite character and claimed them as our boyfriend. Then years later, at a club where I worked, there was a huge celebrity party one night. It was like someone had ripped the page out of a gossip magazine and all of the big names were there. I was used to that and had become pretty unfazed whenever I would meet or wait on famous people. And then I saw him. My "boyfriend" from the movie. My dream guy from my friend's basement. When he walked by me and touched the belt I was wearing, I was almost speechless. The belt was like a belly dancer's and the coins that hung from it jingled as I walked in high-heeled red leather stiletto boots. As his fingers tickled the coins, they responded and so did I:

"You just had to touch it, didn't you?"

"I wanted to see them shake."

"You could've asked."

"I'm asking."

"I'm shaking."

Sometimes you go back in time as soon as a moment has passed and wished you had said something different, something cooler, something more. Not this time. Our banter was immediate. He got my humor and didn't skip a beat. I obliged and did my best little Shakira hip wiggle as he handed me a joint. We began talking and soon found out that he was from a town near mine and would be a few minutes away from where I lived when he went to the dentist the next day. He asked me to meet him at Starbucks for a cup of coffee. I casually said yes and spent the entire cab ride home on a group message deciding on what I would wear, say and order to appear as though a daytime date with my movie boyfriend was no big *thang*.

I never told him that story even after we started hanging out pretty casually whenever he was in my area. It turned into some more intentionally planned booty calls but never anything else. He was very confident and sometimes arrogant. I didn't think that there'd ever really be space in his life for something real and I didn't want to shift the balance we had by being in the "fan" category, so I never gave away that I even knew who he was. But, I think the young girl in me still got such a thrill that my childhood crush turned into my grown up friend-with-benefits that I had a tough time resisting his invitations.

So I said yes. He opened the door to the room without turning on a light.

"Hey."

"Hey."

"You can tell you came from work. You look like sex."

How do you reply to that? So often, when he spoke, I wondered if I should say what I was really thinking or if I was meant to sound more scripted. I never could tell if he ever actually turned the actor part off.

I followed him into the room. We spent the next hour in a sea of sheets. Even if it was a perpetual role that he was playing, he was very talented in being present. He made me feel like a grown-up. A woman. A sex object. And it was empowering to be able to safely step into that feeling. Afterwards, I glanced at the clock. It was late. The bed was comfortable. I was tired. And yet, I got up, went to the bathroom and left. Some guys were sleepover guys. Others weren't. This one wasn't.

CHAPTER THREE

"It is not important what we can do as teachers,
but rather what we show is possible for our students."
—*Tao Porchon-Lynch*

I was covered with dust from pressing my face out the small open window. I couldn't peel my eyes away from the scene that was unfolding outside. The crowded bus raced down the busy street filled with the hustle and bustle of city life. The smells of the exotic food wafting through the window, the colors of the beautiful fabrics being sold on the sidewalks, the sounds of the horns and beggars; it was all so intoxicating. Our driver expertly maneuvered through the mayhem narrowly avoiding every possible kind of vehicle only to screech to a halt for the cow that was walking lazily in the middle of the road. Cars, motorbikes that held entire families, trucks, camels, rickshaws, auto rickshaws and pedestrians were all vying for their slice of the commuter pie. It was only the second day of our trip and India was proving to be a feast for all the senses.

We had stopped at place to eat and shop when we happened upon a sari store. It turned out that this wasn't just any sari shop but Tao's favorite. She said that we wouldn't be going to the "regular places the tourists go." In keeping with her assurances, the owners rolled out the red carpet when they heard that she was arriving with a group of nine of her students. The group consisted of eight women and one man, and except for me all were over 50. I was feeling extra grateful to have the time (thank you makeup career!) and the money (thank you strip club job!) to have this life-changing experience in my 20s. Since the first international trip to Italy years prior, I had an insatiable wanderlust and wanted to experience the food, language, colors and most importantly, the people, in as many countries as possible.

So, when the owner asked me to model the Indian fashion for the group, I was more than game.

"Come here please, young woman. We will show you the many ways that you can wear the sari."

The group kindly cheered me on as I walked over to the thin man who oozed a salesman's charm.

"For you, I have chosen this gorgeous piece in red. Do you like the color?"

Having never loved nor particularly looked good in red, I was surprised to learn that I actually did love it! Standing there in that shop, in full Indian garb, I was mentally transported to the days of Tao's past. Having heard stories forever about her years as a dancer and a model, and having seen the breathtaking photos of her in full regalia, I felt connected to her. I felt connected to India. I even felt connected to this particular sari.

Renee was watching me as I grinned ear to ear. She had inspired many of us to come on the trip by sharing all about "a yoga retreat that Tao was offering to her native land." At the time, I thought it made perfect sense for me. Then that thought was almost immediately replaced with doubt and "realistic" notions about the length, the cost and the timing of the trip. Why do we do that? Why do we replace joy with the opposite: love with fear, confidence with insecurity, excitement with doubt? I remember asking my parents for their advice.

My mom, ever the source of warmth and support, instantly said that I should go. She even briefly contemplated going too until she realized that the timing wouldn't align with the grad school classes that she taught. She also may have remembered the fact that she was scared of bridges, most cars, heights and much of what travel consisted of. The irony of this never escaped me when she would tell people how much she loved to travel! My dad's reaction, however, was a total surprise. Expecting for him to note the cost, the time away from work, the distance, malaria, etc., I was shocked when he told me to go.

"Josie, Tao means so much to you. She's 86 and you have the chance to see India with her and through her eyes. You have to go."

"Really Dad? I thought you'd say that it was so expensive."

"You work. You make money. You'll always make more money. You'll never regret spending on experiences, and this is a once in a lifetime one. I mean Jo, she's 86. You don't know how much longer she'll be doing these trips."

"You're right Dad."

"I know. I'm always right. You're just now starting to realize it."

"Thanks Dad."

"You're welcome Josie. But Josie ... get the malaria shots and brush your teeth with bottled water."

So here I was twirling around in a red sari, before the days of iPhones, as Renee took a photo of me using my "fancy" digital camera.

"Are you going to buy it Joanna?" she asked "I don't know."

"It looks gorgeous!"

"And it feels amazing. Like a queen or some powerful Indian goddess ... but I don't think so. If I could think of a single place where I'd ever wear it, I'd buy it. But I can't. You should buy one, Renee!"

We left the shop empty-handed. Little did I know at the time that red was the sari color that brides wore at Indian weddings.

The day was filled with contrast. We were headed to the Taj Mahal. We were warned by our driver not to give any money to people begging. He prepared us for the fact that we would be passing children asking for money and that we'd be tempted to give, but if we did, we could get swarmed and that wasn't safe. On the ride there, the woman in the seat next to me started complaining about how dirty the country was and began listing all that was wrong with it. I always wondered about the kind of American traveler who visited other countries only to be disappointed by the ways in which it was different from theirs. I thought they were missing the magic. On this ride, if you could see past the first layer of poverty, past the shanty towns and steel hut-like structures, you could see the beauty of the land, the sky, the scenery.

As if sensing my thoughts, Tao touched my arm from across the aisle. "It's beautiful, isn't it?"

"It is."

"It's changed so much since when I was a girl, but it's always so beautiful."

"Were you born around here, Tao? Are we going to see where you're from?"

"Yes, I'll take you there. It's a very special place: Pondicherry, the French part of India. It was very unique. It's the place where I first experienced oneness. You'll love it. We'll also visit Kerala and stay in the hotel that Paul McCartney said was the most beautiful place he'd ever seen. And we'll go to Cochin where there is a mosque, a temple and a church all within one mile of each other."

Listening to Tao speak about the beauty of India was like listening to music, and seeing her face alit with joy was like looking at art. I was so happy just to sit with her. To soak up every drop of the magic she shared. After she had left India for France and England during the war, she became a well-known model. Modeling led to acting and being under contract with MGM. Acting led to writing and producing films and she told me with pride about the films she did highlighting "her India." As a result, some of her lifelong friends in India were very famous actors and government officials. There were times when this came in handy. When teaching the tree pose in class, Tao always told us to put the ball of one foot against the inner thigh of the other leg. (Most teachers demonstrate this posture with the flat foot against the leg.) Her feeling is that by using the ball of the foot rather than the flat foot, the bent knee is lifting and bringing up beautiful energy from the ground like the roots of a real tree. If done with flat feet, she said it was more of a weeping willow. Tao once saw a brochure printed by the Indian government inviting tourists to visit. When she saw a tree pose shown with the flat foot, she contacted them and suggested that they change it. They did. Tao always taught, and exemplified, that if something needed doing that it should be done. And immediately.

The bus stopped. We disembarked from the overly air-conditioned stale air of travel and walked in the blanket-like warmth of Agra.

Some sights are so ingrained in your memory that they become a part of your consciousness. They are so majestic, so powerful that they are fade-proof. The Vatican was one of those places for me. And so was this. Seeing the Taj Mahal in person is indescribable. There are few things in life that are so stunningly, overwhelmingly beautiful that I am rendered speechless.

This was one of those moments.

The sheer magnitude, the beauty, washed over me; austere and warm, grand and detailed. I listened as Tao pointed out aspects I may have otherwise missed and couldn't help but be flooded, once again, with gratitude that I was not only seeing one of the wonders of the world but that I was being guided by one as well.

"Do you feel it? Do you feel the peace?" she asked me.

"I do."

"I know you do. You are special, Dear. Wherever we go, people are drawn to you because you have a smile that radiates love."

"Tao, I'm pretty sure I'm just mirroring you. When you see me, I'm always happy because I'm with you. So you see me at my most present."

"I do see you, Dear. And I've always known, from that first time you came to my class, that we were meant to do things together."

"I'm so grateful to be here with you. I feel so lucky to see India with you."

"Did you see, Dear? Some of the people on the bus only saw the poverty. They were noticing what's missing. So they will find what's missing wherever they go. We decide what we notice, and what we notice grows. So always be careful where you put your attention. And always choose to see the positive. Just beyond the people begging were the most playful monkeys. I hope you saw the monkeys."

We took in every nook and cranny of the Taj Mahal from within before walking around the grounds. As Renee and I traded turns posing in the quintessential tourist pose, the one that made it look to the viewer as though we were holding the tip of the Taj by our fingertips, a small crowd started to gather. Renee and I noticed a group of mostly women who were excitedly speaking amongst themselves while looking at us and pointing.

Was it our imagination? Were we committing some unknown tourist faux pas on sacred ground? My sister had gotten kicked out of her share of churches in Italy for having shorts too short or for not covering her shoulders. Were we inadvertently breaking the rules?

We smiled and were about to walk back to our group when one of the women handed me her baby. I glanced at Renee to see if she was also getting a cute local kid, but her hands remained empty. The small crowd of women seemed to become even more excited when one took out a camera and started taking pictures of her baby and me. Renee started laughing and I couldn't help but smile at what was either the strangest part of my day or a very warm custom that I had never heard of. The baby was cooing as we both said our native tongue's version of cheese. After the pics were snapped, the women began to clap. Thinking the photo session complete, I went to return the baby when I understood one phrase repeatedly mentioned in the midst of the Hindi. One that was universally understood: *"Catherine Zeta-Jones."*

Apparently, what I had considered to be an interesting Indian custom was simply a case of mistaken identity. They totally thought I was Catherine Zeta-Jones! I didn't have the words (nor the desire) to ruin the story that they would surely take back to their local friends telling of their brush with fame. I was also super flattered to be compared to the gorgeous actress so it was a win-win at the Taj. Years later that silly little story would have a funny, full-circle twist. My sister found out that the neighborhood threader she visited also worked on Catherine Zeta-Jones. She told her about the run in at the Taj and she, in turn, told Catherine who got such a kick out of it.

So much magic happened throughout the almost two-week trek through India. We explored the tea plantations of Thekkady where I had the most delicious orange juice I had ever tasted and eggs that were just laid moments before. I rode an elephant down a local street, but it was so commonplace that no one even looked twice. We celebrated New Year's in black tie garb and drank wine curated by Tao. As a celebrated wine judge, she would take the selection of our bottles seriously. In fact, Tao never drank water; only wine, champagne, tea and juice. She taught me that the Sanskrit word for "wine" is the same for "hope" and that where there was wine, there was hope. She loved the strength and fragility of grapes and said how much we could learn from them. She pointed out how different two grapes could be depending on their proximity to sunshine, exposure to rain, etc. Tao loved and appreciated all things in nature and when in her presence, I found myself noticing the beauty in the smallest things too. I could listen to her for hours, and on this trip I got the chance to do that for days in a row.

In Kerala, we experienced the most amazing Ayurvedic treatments, and practiced yoga in the rice paddies overlooking the ocean. In one class, Tao was seated at the front of our "room," which was more of an open-air hut, that provided a feeling of instant peace. Connected to nature and hearing the sounds of the birds and feeling the cool breeze around us, I came into my breath. Tao's words guided me into the present moment:

"Feel nature all around us. And within us. For everything that exists outside of us, also resides within us. Every blade of grass pulsates with the same life force as our breath. We are not the doer. We are the instrument. That which made us, is still in us. So, everything we can envision, we can create. Inhale your arms over your head and move with that breath. Feel it energize you as the sun that rises brightens the sky. It isn't enough to breathe a little bit. Breathe into your fingernails. Breathe into your toes. Each breath is a breath of beginning. Of renewal. And each breath you take in yoga adds a year to your life without pain. Look at me. I plan to make it to at least 100. But I don't just want to make it to 100, I want to dance my way there. I want to teach my way there."

Her voice, her wisdom, her energy. They were the thread and she was weaving her magic into our consciousness. In that space, all that I truly was in my essence, I felt. Anything I no longer needed, was washing away. Loneliness, doubt, and insecurity were hissing their way out of me as would air from a tire punctured by a nail. For too long, I had allowed comparisons to make me feel less than; unfaithful boyfriends to make me feel not enough; and chosen paths to make me feel unsuccessful. Hearing Tao's words—FEELING Tao's words—and the energy behind them, fanned the flames of the fire that she had originally lit years before.

Everything was different in India. One new (non-American) experience was having full-body massages that included the breasts. They had us begin with only "underwear" made of a gauzy material, and after only a few minutes with the healing oils, it was nothing but a memory.

We ate the freshest fish and attended a Kathakali show. We arrived early and watched as they applied the traditional makeup. Men played all the parts so usually the "women" were younger boys with intricate makeup made from natural plants and materials. Most interesting was how the performers used eye movements and facial gestures to act out entire tales. We visited temples and sacred sites. We shopped in colorful and amazing markets which were off the beaten path.

We used every form of transportation and even had an accident in an autorickshaw (think three-wheeled scooter with a driver and room for two.) But still, even after the fender bender, no one stopped for us. They just went on with their day. In one of my favorite hotels, we stayed in five-star "huts" in the backwaters with luxury bathrooms that had no roofs but for the canopy of sky and stars. I loved peeing in the middle of the night and being able to reach out and touch a tree. Sitting by the pool, magical looking houseboats that seemed like they had come out of *Aladdin* would pass through tiny canals throughout the property. I read a book as a cow sunned itself next to me. I daydreamed about being in such a setting with someone I loved. I began to see him with more clarity. In fact, this trip was bringing so much of my life into focus. I often thought when in my 20s and traveling so much that there was something magical about the perspective of distance. On one of my early trips home to New York from visiting Antonio in Italy, I distinctly remember feeling the energy and anxiety from the surrounding passengers on my flight. The stress on their faces as they were taking out computers or papers to work on was palpable. For a moment, I recalled the feeling of feeling like I was supposed to be DOING something or at least FEELING something similar to their anticipatory vibe. I paused. I stopped myself and committed from that day on to always be grateful for feeling happy and present and to choose to not wear busy as a badge of honor. Because the alternative, choosing stress for stress's sake, is utterly ridiculous.

And though we were on the go in Mumbai and in the midst of the hustle and bustle of city life, we also made time for incredible foot massages that cost the equivalent of $13 US. At this point, the juxtaposition of poverty and wealth, of country and city, of ancient and modern was becoming the norm. Each experience was peppered with the intimate stories and colorful past of our Tao. It was here that we had lunch at one of her friend's homes. As a very well-known actress in India, this friend and her family could have lived in a castle. In fact, as we ate incredible homemade food seated casually around their living room, a commercial came on the television showing her in her most famous role. On the elevator ride back down to the bus, Tao shared with me more about her friend. She used her fame to help others. She believed in living on 10 percent of what she earned and giving the rest away. She was single-handedly responsible for teaching the beauty of farming, gardening and agriculture to young school children. With Tao the textures of stories were always as remarkable as the people who surrounded her.

Mumbai (formerly Bombay) was our final stop before leaving for the States. Renee and I were casually sitting by the pool in a luxury hotel, talking about our favorite moments of this magical adventure, when the subject turned to love.

"So, Joanna. What kind of love are you looking for?"

"Oh, that's easy. I know the answer to that one. I have a list."

"A list?"

"Yes. Of course. I wrote a list."

"To the man?"

"No! That'd be crazy."

Renee looked both amused and curious.

"To the universe," I clarified.

"Oh. I see."

"Renee, if you're ready for your forever man, write a list!"

"What'd you put on yours?"

"Everything I'd want in my forever dude."

"How many things are on it?"

"I think about 78."

I went on to share how you have to be specific when placing such an order for the law of attraction works in specificity. (See parking angels for a review) The 78 included the superficial such as over 6'2" with salt and pepper hair and shoulders that didn't slope. Chemistry is important, and if you don't have that you won't notice the deeper and more meaningful aspects. I also put: loves family, likes to travel, is generous and a good listener, and has a range to discuss anything from Buddha to Biggie Smalls. As we chatted, Renee was in equal parts both ready to write her own list and absolutely convinced of my insanity. As we were in the moment of talking about the manifestation of love, a handsome pilot appeared out of nowhere. Renee looked at me and I could instantly read her mind. *Man, the universe works fast!*

It turned out the pilot was a kite surfer from Sri Lanka and he was really interesting. He showed me photographs he took of the world from the cockpit and regaled me with stories of his kite surfing adventures. We spent the afternoon connecting and enjoying each other's company until it was time for me to leave and go find the group. At the exact moment that

I thought he would lean in for the international romance kiss, he said he had a girlfriend.

List man this was not. But with every bit of my soul, I felt he was coming. The universe gives you coming attractions in the movie of your life if you pay attention. I felt like the pilot was my spoiler alert that the real one was on his way.

The experience of traveling through India with both Tao and Renee proved to be life-changing in every sense. Not only did it expand my mind, my heart and my capacity for adventure, but it actually altered my life's path. I expected to create memories that I would always cherish. I expected to be wowed by the country and to enjoy every second of being so close to Tao and sitting at the feet of her wisdom. What I had not planned though was the prescient conversation that happened on the bus to the airport.

It started simply with the topic of the pilot from the night before.

"Was he a nice man, Dear?"

"He was Tao. And smart and kind. A gentlemen."

"Oh good."

"But he has a girlfriend."

"Don't worry, Dear. Your maharaja is coming."

"Thanks Tao."

She touched my face with her soft, strong and perfectly manicured hands. "And he's coming soon."

I asked her how she had met her first husband, the love of her life. She told me about how she was dancing in England when he and his fellow Free French fighter pilot friends would come to see the shows. The story was both heartwarming and heart-wrenching and made modern love seem so relatively simple compared to that of their wartime love.

Glancing over at Tao, I took in her whole look. With a five AM wake-up call, most of the group was outfitted in comfortable travel wear or yoga clothes. Not Tao. She was in leather pants, a colorful top, a glamorous scarf, full makeup and of course her signature high heels. We rode in silence for a few minutes before she turned to me with the thought that would change my life.

"It's time for you to teach yoga."

"I actually have started, Tao. I have a friend who wanted to take it but didn't want to go to a studio, so I started teaching her once a week and she cooks me dinner." I continued casually, "I teach for food."

But she wasn't casual. There was an intensity in her crystal-blue eyes. "That's cute. But it's time for you to really teach."

"Funny, Tao. My mom says the same thing. The last time we went to Kripalu, she told me to go get certified there and that she would pay for it. She thinks I'm meant to spread peace."

"She's right. I want you to continue what I do."

CHILLS!

She wasn't done. "You embody what yoga is. The beauty of life. The connection. The unity. Everything you do, you do with such a smile and wonder. And it isn't false. As I always tell you, even from the first day I met you in class, I knew we were supposed to do something together." There. She said it AGAIN. That SHE felt something the first time we met. I chalked up what I was feeling to what I presumed EVERYONE felt when they met her: awe. Never would I imagine that the serendipitous meeting would be something significant enough for Tao to take notice!

Tears flowed down my cheeks as I listened in stunned silence to these beautiful words from the most beautiful being. I had been following her around, studying with her for years now. She had hundreds of students who respected her wisdom and light. To be singled out in this manner was the biggest honor I had experienced in my life to date.

"It's time for you to get certified and I want to personally do it."

Mic drop.

It was like Yoda telling you to do something. And like Yoda, I knew that if I did this, there would be "no try. Just do."

My eyes shined through the tears as I simply held both of her hands in mine and accepted the responsibility of her faith. Our nods solidified the magic of the moment and my silent tear-filled smile confirmed to her that I had received the message and honor and responsibility that went along with it. Completely filled up, when Tao switched seats to talk to the one man on our tour, I rested my head on the window and closed my eyes to imagine the story she had been telling me about meeting her husband before we got on the topic of teaching yoga. Inspired by both Gandhi and her aunt, Tao was committed to doing what she could to help as many people as possible during the war. To entertain the troops and bring some joy into a world of fear, she had put together new dance shows and performed them many times each night in different clubs around London. Fearing that that wasn't enough, she actually became a part of the resistance. Using her shows as cover, Tao would partake in secret missions to France to help sneak people to safety. Concealed under sacks of potatoes to mask their human scent from the dogs, they used fishing boats and a tunnel system under Paris to make their escape. Though it wasn't something she shared with many people, being a part of the resistance was very important to Tao. Along with so many others, she used the fact that she was a woman and a performer to hide her courageous acts in plain sight.

But after her friend was caught and tortured, it became too dangerous for Tao to continue and she returned to England. Horrified by the thought of her friend having suffered so much before he was killed, she took some solace in the notion that she had done her small part to be a piece of a larger movement. Tao always believed that when you saw an injustice, it wasn't enough to hope for better. It was necessary to ACT for better. One night when she was back to performing in London in her typically ambitious nightly schedule, a group of French fighter pilots entered the nightclub. Each man had a woman that they were hoping to meet. Tao saw one man who stood out from the rest. Small in stature but tall in the pride he clearly felt wearing his uniform, she thought he was the most handsome man she had ever seen. When she asked him who he had come to meet, he replied that he was already looking at her.

So began the story of Tao's greatest love. Yvan was smart, brave and funny. Much to the amusement of his fellow fighters, he would yodel when going into combat. While the element of fear existed every time they would part, she chose to focus on the joy they'd experience with each reunion. So many of her friends were losing their lives that Tao couldn't help but feel grateful for each of the times that Yvan would return. It was a time filled with heightened senses: love and death, joy and impermanence. On one trip, Yvan told Tao that the next time he came back, they would get married.

They did.

After France was liberated, Yvan and Tao lived as a married couple in Paris. Those were years she would remember fondly for the rest of her days. Even decades later, Tao's eyes had an extra sparkle when she would spoke of Yvan. Their love had romance, humor, adventure and passion. And like many such love stories, it had an ending.

CHAPTER FOUR

"I wake up every single day and just know it's going to be the best day of my life."
—*Tao Porchon-Lynch*

"Connect your thumb and your first finger. But don't be dainty when you use Mudras—these are powerful hand gestures that connect your physical selves with the spiritual. Be on purpose. Lift your arms as you inhale. Feel that inhale fill every bit of your body, expand your heart and radiate that joy from there. Now exhale as you bring your palms together and bring it back down to the heart center. That matching up of breath and movement is the dance of life within you. Each sun salutation is a way of greeting this new day and that newness brings infinite possibilities. As you walk through busy marketplaces in India early in the morning, the sun rises and people stop shopping and do a sun salutation. When I was a little girl, I used to love looking at their different versions and would know from what part of India they came by the way they practiced. For people in the mountains experienced the first glimpse of the new day differently than those in other areas. The breath is the link: the vinyasa. And as you move from one pose to another, your breath flows into the next ..."

As always, in a class with Tao, I found myself transfixed, hanging on her every word. I wasn't listening to what she said as much as I was feeling it in the depths of my soul. Her classes were like sun shining inside of me and as I moved through the physical practice, I began gliding on my breath. By the end, she demonstrated her signature shoulder stand. Considered the "queen of all asanas" or physical poses, a shoulder stand is a powerful inversion which brings your legs up into the air. Often when people practice this pose, the natural tendency is to have the legs be over head. Tao taught us to challenge ourselves to keep the legs over the hips instead. She then showed us her nightly routine which included several leg variations as well as pressing the legs away from the head even farther and then returning them to be over the hips. This appeared deceptively simple, but in reality required way more core strength than I currently had. This was class with Tao: watching her do seemingly impossibly feats and then seeing and feeling her belief that you, too, could do the same. The magical fairy dust she sprinkled always seemed to work. And in my next attempt, I managed to do the variation she was teaching.

As we were rolling up our mats, Tao approached me for our post-class hug.

"Thank you, Tao. That was a beautiful class as always."

"Oh good, Dear. I hope I didn't bore people today." This wasn't false humility. Having no basis for comparison, she truly didn't seem to grasp just how extraordinary her life and her teaching was.

"You couldn't bore people if you tried, Tao!"

"I know we spent a lot of time on the shoulderstand at the end. But it's important that people do the correct form so they can feel the power of their breath."

"Tao, I can assure you … people may leave here empowered or exhausted or both. But no one ever leaves a class with you bored!"

At this point, she touched my face with her wrinkled yet strong hands and perfectly polished nails. Standing face to face with her as she was putting on her signature heels, I couldn't help but notice for the umpteenth time just how much light and energy could be contained in such a petite package.

"You are always so sweet with me."

"I'm so happy to be with you Tao. I've missed seeing you every day since we came back from India. It was such a special trip. Thank you again."

"I'm so happy you came. And I hope you thought over what we talked about. I want to certify you to start teaching."

"I have thought about it and I'm going to definitely do it."

"Oh good. You know what I always say … procrastination is the only sin."

"Well don't worry. I'm ready to start right away."

"Good. Now … have you met your maharaja yet?"

I couldn't contain the laugh that erupted. "Tao, we've only been back a week. I didn't expect the universe to work that fast."

"Why not? The universe delivers in direct relation to how ready we are to receive." She paused and got more serious as she looked over my face and took a breath. "Your maharaja is coming."

I let the smile fill my face.

"And he's coming soon."

"May I have an iced chai but without the ice?"

The barista looked confused until Jahari came out from the back. She had already become accustomed to my twice-weekly order. I wanted the energy when my shift at the club started. If we added the ice when I ordered it, it would melt into a cup of watery, flavorless nasty by the time I got into the city. I had learned this by trial and error over the past two years of Tuesday/Thursday shifts. Jahari took over. She once told me that working at Starbucks was one of three jobs she managed to fit in around going to school. At fifteen, she was harder working and more disciplined than most adults. A year prior, she was admiring my phone and I told her that I had just gotten an upgrade. That's when she asked if I would sell her my old one. When I came in the next day to give her the phone as a gift, she teared up. From that moment on, she made sure that none of the fellow baristas charged me for my chai. Appreciative and a bit uncomfortable with the arrangement, I began to put the money straight into the tip box instead.

"You look beautiful today."

"Thanks Jahari. You're probably the only person that would understand my look."

"Why? Most people wear full runway-ready makeup with a tank top, sweatpants and sneakers." At this point, she acted out an over-the-top pretend runway walk from the espresso machine to the pastry display.

"I'm like a mullet. Fancy up top and cas below."

"But seriously, Jo. Your makeup is extra on point today. Like fire! Are you doing something special after work? Or is a special customer coming in? You know I love your celebrity sightings! TELL ME! Is it the actor?"

On days like this, when there was no line of people waiting for their afternoon hits of caffeine, we would chat about all the madness that happened at the club. A steady *US Weekly* reader, Jahari loved the inside scoop.

"Sorry to disappoint love. But I got nothing. Just a regular Tuesday."

"I don't know ... there's something about you today."

"Well in that case, I'll take it. If you're feeling magic, I'll go with that. When life offers magic, TAKE IT!"

She handed me my iced, non-iced drink and I left with a smile.

The ride into Manhattan on the West Side Highway was the perfect way to transition. Leaving the grassy suburbs of Westchester for the concrete madness of the city was part of it. Each time I would go over the toll that separated the Bronx from Manhattan, I would choose lane 13. The one and three always reminded me of my Mommom whose birthday was the 31st. They had become my magical numbers, the numbers that guided me. Most of us, if we pay attention, have numbers that seem to always be on the clock when we look or on the license plate in front of us or of the date of a meaningful event. So each time through lane 13 I was reminded to have a quick chat with my Ladybug. Sometimes it was a simple wish, a prayer or just an *I miss you.* On this particular ride, I found myself being influenced by my conversation with Jahari.

Hi Mommom. I miss you always. Please bring me magic today and the presence to notice it ....

...Often, the mundane becomes meditative. Each of the private champagne rooms required the same setup. Six champagne flutes. The silver bucket. The maroon cloth napkin. The napkin was spread in the shape of a triangle on the small table. The bucket was placed at the back and the six glasses formed a "V" just like the napkin. During the previous three years, I had mastered the skill of carrying all six flutes in one trip. When you made about seventy trips from the bar to the rooms each night, this skill was more important than one might presume. Returning from finishing the last room, I was surprised to see Lisa, my fellow waitress partner in crime for the night. I love Lisa. She is a beautiful person, inside and out. And so thin that she was able to continue working while secretly pregnant without anyone suspecting a thing. What was one more secret in a place that was filled with lies, scandal and dark behavior? Typically posted in the downstairs VIP area on Tuesdays, I did a double take when I saw her sit down for family meal.

The chef fed us well but considering where we worked and what we did, each night we had the same question. Why was it all garlic and carbs? Opting for the least offensive choices, I quickly ate, competed in a pre-shift ritual of a sudoku challenge with a waiter from the steakhouse, and changed. "Changing" was easy. I pulled the micro skirt over my sweats and then peeled the pants off from underneath. I swapped the tank top for the blazer that was tight and fitted and showed more than a hint of lacy bra underneath. I rubbed some oils in strategic places and some bronzing lotion on my legs. Then I sat to lace up the shoes around my ankles. I remembered reading that on *Seinfeld* the character who played Kramer wore the same shoes for every single episode. I thought of that as I tied the lace around my second ankle. Standing up, I went for the final touches; a light gloss on my lips and the black rimmed glasses that I didn't really need. The ones "for the sex, Banana"—my childhood nickname had sounded so different when it rolled off of Antonio's accented tongue. The lights dimmed. The music came on. I put the ice in my chai. The doors opened. The floor manager who covered the private rooms and the restaurant said the same thing he did at the start of every shift: "Alright everybody. Boys, get ready. Girls, tits out."

Tits out. That was his vile way of telling us to face the stairs from where the first customers would arrive. Every single time I heard these words, I cringed. Having just returned from my life-changing adventure in India, I couldn't believe that I still worked in a place where hearing "tits out" was normal.

The early shift typically started off slow. When you opened and worked from four PM to two AM, you traded some of the late-night debauchery for some early evening boredom. The restaurant would get a rush and we waitresses would handle the pre-table cocktails until the guests were seated. It was a good routine because by the time they finished eating, they would drunkenly reconnect with us as if we were old friends. As dining wound down around 11:00, the champagne rooms would be in full swing and we would be running from room to room, bottle to bottle. We loved the bottles and were told to push them. Not only was the markup absurd for the club and we'd get a

20 percent gratuity on all bottles ordered, but it also kept the customers busy longer. Either in the spirit of generosity or by nature of being embarrassed by what we had witnessed them do in the privacy of the rooms, the customers would usually tip on top of the already included service charge. So the time of closing out the checks was when we really put on the charm.

The restaurant was beginning to fill up. It didn't take much for this to happen. The top floor of the club was shaped like a rectangle with the inside of the rectangle cut out to see the main floor below. The two long sides were filled with booths and tables and comprised the steakhouse. The back area that connected the two sides held three private rooms named for their colors: the Red Room, Black Room and Silver Room. The Black Room, being the largest, held the most people and cost the most to rent by the hour. On the side opposite of those three rooms was the bar, the kitchen, another private room and an area of tiny Morrocan-styled booths for rent called the Harem Rooms.

We schmoozed and greeted all the guests as they waited for their tables. We made sure everyone had their cocktail of choice. On any given night, there were familiar faces and the wide-eyed telltale look of the first timers. Lisa had one group of guys all give her kisses as they filed in. Sometimes when this happened, we knew them. Other times, customers acted like they knew us just to look like regulars in front of their clients or friends. It was all such a game.

Having a lull in drink delivery, Lisa and I started talking with the bartender, who was a recovering alcoholic named Charlie, about dating. Charlie was an actress who made some of the best drinks in the club, even though she never tasted them. When a customer wanted to buy her a drink, she would charge them and make herself a "mocktail" instead. Having perfected a drink that looked like the alcoholic counterpart of anything ordered, she could fool anyone. It was her way of being able to mingle, flirt and earn big tips without compromising her sobriety. Yet another small drop of deception in an ocean of pretense.

As we gossiped about different men, Lisa turned her attention to me. "When are you going to start dating?"

"I date."

"No, I mean for real. Who was the last guy you dated?"

"Scientist."

"Scientist?"

"Yep. He was so nice."

"Too nice?"

"More like nice in the wrong way. Like DAD nice. So smart and really sweet but like tall white socks and sandals kind of nice."

"Ugh. Done. Who'd you go out with before that?"

At this point, Charlie chimed in. "Wasn't Navy SEAL before Scientist?"

"Oh my God, yes! I almost forgot about him."

Back to Lisa. "So ... what happened with Navy SEAL? That sounds sexy."

"It was. And manly and impressive and mysterious. But not a real thing."

"Why? That's so hot."

Charlie popped her head up from the small dishwasher. "You may want to hook up with Jason Bourne. But no girl wants to marry that."

Probably due to equal parts of boredom and genuine interest, Lisa didn't relent. "You never come out with us. You're not going to meet your next man at home on your couch. Stop being such a dork."

She was part of the crew that would actually go to other clubs after ours closed. Always excited about which DJ would be spinning at which place, her late-night group kept the party going. That is before her surprise bun in the oven, when she was queen of that crew. And she was right. I wanted nothing to do with those nights.

"I should hook you up with one of my friends."

Mentally reviewing the guys that I had seen Lisa with up until this point, I ruled them out as being a match. I didn't think anyone in that "go out" world would be into me or that I would be into anyone so interested in "seeing and being seen."

"Thanks love. But I'm super picky."

"Obviously."

Saved by the little fingertip wave beckoning a waitress to their table—the universal gesture of "I need something"—I went to take care of a small group of stockbrokers. From that moment until about two hours later, we were lost in the dance of service: opening tabs, flirting, taking orders, chatting, pushing bottles, deflecting grabby hands.

And closing out checks. I was bringing the check to a guy in the Silver Room to expedite the subtle process of kicking him out and turning the room over quickly. The customers were charged hundreds of dollars per hour just for the room so when their time had expired, no dust was able to settle before the next group willing to pay could be brought in. I had learned that the tips were significantly higher if you closed the tab while they were still in the room and still in the party mode. It seemed the moment they stepped outside of the room, the fantasy was already fading and they were more likely to give a "realistic" tip as opposed to a "show off-ey" one. This time I may have overcorrected and walked in while the party was a bit too much in full swing. As soon as I entered, I noticed the room was darker than usual and saw that they had taken the cloth napkins and draped them over the sconces.

In the faded light, I could see the main guy, the one who had ordered all the bottles of champagne, waving me over. He had a topless dancer perched on one leg and another behind him massaging his shoulders. As I knelt to hand him the bill, he pulled me onto his lap. The dancer on the other leg was one of the girls I really liked. She was a professional and would work a customer so expertly that he would feel that their connection was real even while handing over piles of money to pay her for her time. She also made sure that any bartender, floor host, waitress or security guy got tipped. On one of the quieter nights, she had shared with me about having a son she was raising on her own while going to school during the day. Only pretending to be a party girl, she was sober every night. Which meant she ordered often and ordered expensively. When she saw me hand the guy his bill, she grabbed it from my hand. "Baby you got your hands full. Why don't I do this?"

"Look at this service," he laughed.

"We have to take care of my girl."

"Okay. Put an extra $100 on there on top of the service then."

She looked at me and winked as she stroked his hair, and his ego.

"Oh, come on baby. You can do better than that. Let's just add a zero."

"Well, how can I refuse when I'm sitting here with two gorgeous girls on my lap and one rubbing my shoulders?"

Peeling myself off his leg, I gave him the pen to sign his name and took the bill. On the way out, I nodded to the security guy at the door signaling that the customer had paid and that he could now tell him his time was up. He grabbed me on the arm as I was passing. Expecting his usual order of Diet Coke with no ice, Grady instead said that they'd just walkied him to tell me I was needed at the bar.

With a bounce in my step and $1,000 tip in hand, I saw Lisa at the service station. Since we pooled our tips, I was excited to tell her that this night was on track to be a good one. When I looked at her face and saw the smile taking up most of it, I figured that she also had a good table or room to report. "Jo! Guess what?"

"The stockbrokers ended up doing bottles?"

"No. They were cheap bastards. Individual drinks and so loud and annoying."

"Ugh. But don't worry Lisa. The Silver Room was awesome. A $1,000 on top of the bottles. So tonight will be good no matter what."

"Tonight will be more than good. I HAVE THE PERFECT GUY FOR YOU!"

"Oh God."

"And he's here! I can't believe I never thought of him. He's so perfect for you. I've known him forever and he's a REALLY good guy. And he's nice."

"Who is it?"

"That guy. Over there. The tall guy in the black shirt."

"Wow." I was impressed.

"What?"

"I noticed that guy the second he walked in." As soon as he had walked up the stairs and passed the light wall with images of naked women, I thought how handsome he was. But that was right as the Silver Room was booked and I got too busy to check him out. "Physically, he's exactly my type." He had to be at least 6'4" which meant I could wear heels as high as I wanted and he'd still be taller than me. He had the broad shoulders that I loved, salt and pepper hair and the most gorgeous face. His features seemed almost perfect but somehow still manly

"Shut up! So, should I introduce you?"

"I don't know." We had always joked about how unlikely it would be to find something real in a place so artificial. "Let me watch him first."

So I did. He was striking and when he spoke to his friends, his face lit up with animation; with excitement. He didn't seem to be overly interested in the dancers. Sometimes customers paid the women to sit and have dinner with them for the conversation. Other times, particularly when it was slower, the dancers approached the men as they ate. They would offer lap dances in between courses or simply try to impress the customer enough that they would look for that specific woman when they were done with their meal. Either way, a table for 10 of younger, better-looking guys drew a lot of attention. But the salt and pepper man seemed to be annoyed when the ladies approached him. His focus was on his friends and his steak.

When the security guy closest to me radioed to remind me of Grady's Diet Coke with no ice, I was brought back to the present. From that moment, I became lost in the sea of service once again. Two hours later, I got back to the bar and Lisa grabbed my hand enthusiastically.

"Finally! He's waiting for you. His friends all wanted to go but I made him wait. Come on!"

With no time to retouch my lip gloss or even glance at one of the many mirrors on the walls, I half jogged in my heels to keep up with her. Slightly out of breath, Lisa pulled me right up to the tall, broad-chested guy that I was only hours before semi stalking.

"Jo, this is Mike. Mike, this is Jo."

CHAPTER FIVE

*"When that first ray of sun hits my face in the morning, I know that like
everything in nature, I have just been regenerated, renewed, reborn."*
—Tao Porchon-Lynch

After the war, Tao was becoming well known in Europe and had become
the preferred model of a few couture designers. Having dresses fitted to her
specific measurements and modeling them for high society and royalty was
a part of her life filled with glamor. But as it was getting easier for Tao
professionally, it was getting harder for Yvan. It was difficult for him and
some other fighter pilots to find work. Those who flew the bigger planes
found jobs with airlines. Those who didn't, struggled. At first, this chasm
in their marriage seemed small. Over time, it became more of a divide and
he decided that he should pursue the possibility of employment in South
America. Feeling that supporting both of them would add to his burden, Tao
stayed back to continue her career. If she kept modeling and performing, she
could earn enough money to follow Yvan without him having the pressure
of providing for them both.

Tao was prepared to work. She was prepared to do what was necessary.
What she wasn't prepared for was the loneliness. Often apart throughout the
war, she thought this new separation would feel the same, but it didn't. He felt
so much farther away. So much more gone. Since they were lucky that he had
even survived when so many of their friends had perished, she felt silly and
ungrateful fretting over their distance from one another. She would quickly
tell herself to snap out of it and focus on what was within her control. She
continued to find comfort in her work and in her friends.

The famous movie star Marlene Dietrich was one of the friends who
always brought Tao both courage and laughter. Once, after Tao had finished

acting in a small part in a film, Marlene threw a party in her honor. She told Tao what to wear and how to look sophisticated, and even lent her a fancy cigarette holder. Tao, strikingly beautiful, entered the party at the top of a staircase and with all eyes on her, proceeded to slip down the flight of stairs. At first embarrassed, her spirits immediately lifted as Marlene approached. "Tao, darling, what an entrance! I must use that for my next film." She and Marlene had so much in common in their friendship founded on mutual courage, strength and authenticity.

Few people could see beyond the smile and the sparkle in her eye, to the emptiness that was left in the wake of Yvan's departure. Men wasted no time in trying to get closer to her, but they were of little interest to Tao. She continued to model, perform and travel.

When Tao was specifically requested to be one of a handful of models to go to America, she was thrilled. Assuming that America was closer to Yvan, she reveled in the thought of lessening the distance to her beloved. After a stint in New York, she made her way across the country to Hollywood on a Greyhound bus. Having met people from California in Europe, she hoped that going closer to those contacts and being in the place where films were made would make getting work easier. It did, however her desire to perform was also matched by her passion for social justice.

While traveling, Tao was appalled to see a young, pregnant Black woman having to stand while all the men around her had seats. Always disheartened by injustice, she could not watch any longer. First, Tao suggested that the men act gentlemanly and offer the woman their seat. They quickly shot her down and tried to shut her up. Undeterred, Tao approached the driver who quickly warned that she not get involved in what could be a dangerous matter. Still determined to right the wrong, she personally gave her seat to the pregnant woman. At the next stop, while freshening up, Tao returned to the bus to find all of her belongings, passport and identification included, gone. Despite this, she had always believed and taught that life was not about what happened to you but how you responded. She was committed to always doing what was right even when it wasn't the easy path. And in true Tao way, she expected some good to come out of the situation.

Expect miracles and miracles show.

So when the bus arrived in California, there was a police car at the station. The police officer was one of the people Tao was hoping to see in California! With so few contacts in America, to "happen upon" one of them would seem like an incredible act of fate to some. But to Tao, this is how life could and should be for everyone. She expected the good to come and was grateful and delighted when it did.

Within a short period of time, she was under contract with MGM to act in films. A bit limited by her ability to speak English fluently and by the nature of her exotic look, Tao was often cast as an ethnic character in the background. Although she thought of Yvan constantly, she was also able to make some good, solid friends. When she wasn't working, she would wander into the desert alone and commune with nature. The animals around her, sky above her and sound of the elements all filled her soul with connection and possibility.

A few months into this new life in California, she woke with a feeling of dread and knew in every fiber of her being that something was wrong with Yvan. She was able to reach his mother by mail who confirmed that he hadn't been well and encouraged Tao to come back to meet him in France. She also, strangely, asked Tao to promise that no matter what, she wouldn't leave him. Confused, Tao started to wonder how she could make this happen, when unexpectedly a wealthy friend generously offered to pay for the voyage.

While sailing to Europe, word spread on the boat about Tao being a performer which led to her being recruited to do some shows en route. Performing was never a chore for her. In fact, spreading peace and joy and connecting with people helped take her mind off of her worries about Yvan.

The moment she saw him, she knew something had changed. There was a reluctance in his smile, a hesitation in his hug. While in Uruguay, Yvan grew sick and a young woman began to nurse him. She became infatuated with him. As he told Tao this news, she was quick to say that after three years apart, she could hardly blame him for sleeping with another woman. She was sure that being together would heal all wounds. But he went on to say that the woman was pregnant and had traveled with him to Paris. She was afraid that if she didn't accompany him, that he wouldn't get a divorce. Yvan looked gutted. Facing the love of his life, he sadly asked for a divorce so that he could marry the woman and save her from the shame and disgrace an unmarried pregnancy would bring. Tao obliged and shakily went to the courthouse where she signed the papers ending her marriage to the only man she had ever loved. She put on a brave face and returned to the US with her freshly broken heart.

This was the whole story of her big love and I was honored that she shared it with me on the plane home from India. In light of all the wisdom and history I learned in India about the country and about Tao, this heartbreaking love story was something I hadn't thought as much about as I casually went about my daily life until I was standing in her apartment before we left for her celebratory birthday luncheon. The black and white image of a handsome young man in uniform was prominently displayed on the table in her living room. When I asked if that was her first husband, Tao simply stroked his face and smiled. It was the only time I ever remember seeing sadness in Tao's smile, yet she still shined decked out in a gorgeous blue sari and huge sparkly earrings.

The glass clinked as I tapped it with the knife, quieting the room as I stood for the birthday toast:

"Why wear flats when you can wear heels?

Why drink water when you can drink champagne?

Why walk when you can dance?

Why frown when you can smile?

Today, as we celebrate our Tao, I'm honored to share those questions as just a few of the many I've learned to ask. Tao, I can safely speak for everyone gathered in this room today when I say that our lives are brighter because you're in them. Happy Birthday. We love you so much."

We were celebrating 86 years of magic, inspiration and light. After hugging Tao, I kissed her cheek and returned to my seat. My mom sitting to my right was beaming from ear to ear. My biggest fan, she loved hearing me speak publicly even if it was only a one-minute toast to my mentor. When Ellen Degeneres started her talk show, I always noticed how the camera showed her mom in the audience every day. I completely related to that. Having finished my yoga teacher training with Tao, I had begun teaching my own classes. Bo would show up to every single one and place her mat right in the front. As I would teach, she would wave to me and blow me kisses. I usually made a joke about her being my mom to prevent the assumption that I had a yoga stalking creepster in the front row.

On my left sat my now officially-boyfriend-status dude, Mike. After meeting him that night at work, he called me for the first time a few days later. I was in Florida sitting poolside with my sister and one-year-old niece when my cell phone rang.

"Hello."

"Hey, what's up? It's Mike, Lisa's friend. I met you at the club the other night."

"Oh hey. Good thing you clarified. I gave my number to a lot of Mikes that night."

"That's cool. At least I'm in the running."

We began the usually awkward small talk portion of our first phone call. Only in this case, it wasn't boring. After a few minutes, I gave him the warning that I thought he deserved.

"So, since your friends with Lisa, I should probably warn you now."

"Uh oh. What?"

"I'm not that cool."

He laughed.

"No, I'm serious. I'm kind of dorky. I don't really go out often. I'm not a big 'see and be seen' kind of girl. I work at the club because I needed more taxable income for my mortgage. And every six months, to undo what I see there, I go on a yoga retreat by myself. I just got back from India."

Silence. Then, "India?" His voice changed.

"Yes. I went with my yoga teacher and a small group. She's from there and showed us all around."

Clearly taken aback, he continued. "India. India?"

Oh God, PLEASE let him be smart! I had specifically written smart as one of the criteria on my list to the universe, I thought to myself. "Yes. India."

"It's just really weird, hun. Really weird. I've never even met anyone our age who's ever been to India before."

His response was starting to feel strange, I also hadn't met anyone my age who'd been, so I kept things going. "It was magical."

"Where'd you go?"

"To see the Taj, to the mountains, the south, the tea plantations."

"No, hun. Where in India did you go, specifically?"

I answered with a list of cities.

"So funny."

"Why? Have you been to India?"

"Um, yeah. My dad's Indian and I've gone at least fourteen times. The last time was for my sister's wedding."

At this point, I began to frantically signal my sister who was busy with my niece Jada in the pool.

Playing it cool, I inquired, "Did she marry an Indian guy?"

"No, she married an Italian guy from Westchester. They got married in New Jersey and then six months later, my parents threw them a wedding in India."

I was freaking out! Holding the phone away from my ear, I started emphatically mouthing to my sister HOLY SHIT! THIS IS CRAZY! THIS IS MY HUSBAND! JEN, I'M GOING TO MARRY THIS GUY. OH MY GODDDDDDDD. Then I returned the phone to my ear: "That's so interesting."

On that first call, I knew I would marry him. By the second date, I would have said yes if he had proposed. It had nothing to do with his gorgeous looks. Well, maybe it had a little to do with his gorgeous looks. It wasn't the "coincidence" or "god wink" of the Indian connection. Though in my teachings from Tao, I had come to recognize that when you received signs of coincidence or connection, it was the universe bringing you everything you need. The more you notice it, the more it happens. Even my friends at work were floored when they asked how the first date went. Waiting to hear what his nickname would be (usually it was simply what they did i.e., "Actor," "Scientist," "Navy SEAL," etc.), they were visibly surprised when I answered that this one was different. This was My Dude. And I knew he was different from the very start, because being with Mike felt like being home. The warmth of a hug, the coziness of a fireplace, the safe feeling of being together. It was a sensation I had never experienced and I just knew I had met my forever.

After he took me as his date to a family member's wedding and we stayed overnight partying with his family at a hotel, I told him I was now his girl-friend. He agreed.

I began bringing him more deeply into my world and into my heart by introducing him to my Tao at her birthday party. Always happy to be in the company of kind people, good looking men, or especially both, she was instantly smitten with Mike.

Taking his hand in both of hers, she smiled into his eyes. "It's so lovely to meet you. I have heard wonderful things about you."

Bending down to accommodate her gaze, he responded. "Joanna speaks so highly of you, Tao."

"She's very sweet." She took one hand off his to touch my cheek and include me in the moment. "She's so good to me. And her mother too." Tao looked at my mom with love and Bo looked like she might just jump out of her seat in delight at the beauty of the moment.

Mike continued, "Happy birthday Tao. I'm honored that I get to be here and celebrate with you."

"I'm happy to have you here, Dear. And I can celebrate you two."

I silently prayed. *PLEASE DON'T SAY IT. PLEASE DON'T SAY IT.*

"I hear your father is from India."

PHEW.

"Yes, he is. From Chennai."

"That's right near where I'm from. I'm from Pondicherry. Have you been to Kerala?"

"No. I never went to Kerala. But Jo said that was her favorite so I'm sure we'll be going."

"Yes, and when you do, I will come for the wedding."

OH JEEZ.

Nothing like a guy hearing about his wedding to a girl he'd just started dating! Luckily though, as with most things, normal rules didn't seem to apply to Tao, and she got away with it. I smiled through it and pretended something my mom was saying had suddenly gotten all of my attention.

CHAPTER SIX

"Questions are like jewels. So never be afraid to ask a question.
I have learned more from the questions of my students than I have from the Masters."
—*Tao Porchon-Lynch*

I was born in the 70s and so was a child of the 80s. That means my child-hood was filled with station wagons, lots of hairspray, neon everything and no helmets. I remember being in the back of my mom's station wagon and thinking that independence—I mean true freedom—was facing backwards without a seatbelt on and scream-singing *Hey Mickey you're so fine* at the top of my lungs. To this day, whenever I look out the window of any moving vehicle: plane, train, car, or boat, I feel a spark of imagination and a desire to daydream.

As Tao and I pulled away from the station, I opened my bag of snacks. Mike had dropped us off for our weekend away at the ashram and we walked (or I walked and Tao floated in her requisite heels—that day's selection being strappy and lavender-colored) to the correct platform. Now seated cozily on the train, I started eating trail mix and gazing outside.

"Are you hungry Dear?"

"A little bit. I didn't have time for breakfast this morning. Would you like some nuts, Tao?"

"No thank you. I'm happy just being here on this train with all these beautiful people and the scenery out the window."

I looked out the window again. So far, the view was pretty urban. In fact, I don't think we had seen a bit of green yet. But that's the beauty of the beholder. Tao could see the gift of anything and in anyone.

"And I'm happy to be with you, Dear."

"That's how I feel, Tao. It's such an honor to assist you on a retreat."

"I have a lot of beautiful students. And all the teachers I train I consider to be my children. But you are a special one. From the beginning, I knew you would go out and teach. A lot of people who come through my teacher training aren't looking to teach. They are looking to go deeper within in their own practice. That's good too. But you have been ready to teach from the beginning. And, besides, I'm happy when I'm with you. You're always smiling."

"I'm always smiling when I'm with you because I'm so happy to be with you."

"That's sweet, Dear. But yours is a smile of a young person who wants to do good in this world. And a young person who is in love."

"I am. I am SO in love. You were right about him being my maharaja."

"I bet when the world sees him, they notice how handsome he is. I see something so much more. There is a sweetness and an elegance to him. He looks at you with kindness. And it was so nice of him to drop us this morning. I hope it wasn't too much trouble."

"Are you kidding? He knows how excited I am about going with you. Also, we started living together Tao. So now he knows how much I talk. He's probably excited for a weekend of quiet." Tao loved talking about joy and love and I loved seeing how such conversations brought out her playfulness.

"So ... when are you getting married?"

"Not yet. Let's wait and let him think it's his idea."

"Good approach, Dear. Men like to think it's their idea."

Looking back toward the window, we were heading out of the city and starting to see the landscape shift to sprawling fields and beautiful trees. I could feel how this invigorated Tao. She was so connected to nature that being in or around it instantly recharged her. She was just pointing out how the old winding roots of a tree we were passing were reminders of how powerful the energy was that connected us to the earth and to one another, when we were interrupted: "Good afternoon young ladies."

I looked up to see a man who worked on the train standing over us and started to rifle through my bag for the tickets.

He saw me and quickly clarified, "I don't need to see tickets ma'am."

MA'AM! OMG! Did I just get ma'am-ed!!! In my 20s?!?!?! Did I need eye cream already? I silently told myself *he must have meant that for Tao so refocus girl!*

"I'm sorry to interrupt ma'am." This time he was gazing directly at Tao, so I decided that he just said ma'am all the time and that it was no reflection of my aging. Either that, or maybe he was southern? I'd have to listen for the confirming "y'all" to determine that. He bent down in the aisle to be more at eye level with Tao before continuing.

"I've been working these trains for a while and I've seen a lot of people come and go. When you got on before, I noticed you. It may sound strange, but I saw this, I don't know how to explain it ... I saw a kind of light around you."

"Thank you, Dear. There is a light around you too, you know?"

"Thank you, ma'am. I'm sure people must say this to you all the time but there's something special. Are you, like, a ..."

"People are so sweet. Really. But there is magic in us all."

"Are you two related?" he asked as he glanced at me. "Is this your grand-daughter? Are you going on vacation?"

Okay. Now we're talking. The granddaughter effectively canceled out the ma'am. Did I mention I loved this guy? "We're going to an ashram in Virginia. She's leading a yoga workshop and I'm assisting her. We're not related, at least not by blood."

He absorbed what I was saying as his smile grew. After years of seeing this, it never got old. Tao had an immediate and amazing impact on those she met. As they spoke to her, she lit up. As she spoke to them and focused her light in their direction, they lit up. I would watch and feel these ener-getic fields of connection expand. Her effect was like watching a plant being watered. People would perk up, get closer, shine brighter. And they always wanted, needed, to know more.

He looked at me with intensity. "A yoga workshop? She's a teacher?"

"Not just any teacher. She's a Master teacher."

"Yes. I teach yoga. I could teach you some, you know. You must stand all day and you probably take all the tickets with the same hand. I could teach you to breathe in a way so that you don't get tired. And to switch hands when you take the tickets so that your back and hips stay in alignment."

"Wow. I don't know about that. I'm not flexible. I don't know if I can do yoga. But I would if you were teaching. I don't even know how to explain it. You're like a monk or something. Or like a witch. But a good one. There's just some magic in you."

I totally understood as he struggled to articulate the indescribable light and energy he felt by being around Tao for the first time.

"How old are you, young man?"

"Young man?" He laughed. "I'm 48."

"You are a baby. I'm 87 and I'm just getting started. Remember that with your smile and your curiosity, you have the power to change the world. Just look at what you're doing for all the people on this train today. You greeted everyone with love. You made sure to look at each person and I saw you helping that woman with her baby. You can change the world right where you are. With what you have. And you are already doing that."

At this point, the chatty man went silent. I noticed a sheen in his eyes and realized how deeply Tao's words had touched him. This happened all the time in all different settings. She was always showing how connection, true connection, was not only possible, but necessary, wherever you are.

The man was about to stand and walk away when she reached out her hands. He took her small hands in his and could hardly speak. He was a big man in both height and stature and suddenly, as he connected with Tao, he seemed so innocent. He smiled, looked directly into her eyes and whispered a thank you. Her smile expanded and she released his hands. Touching his cheek, she said she loved him, and he continued walking to the next car.

Before being with Tao, I would have thought it strange to profess love to a stranger. After studying with her for years though, I grew to see that there really isn't such a thing as someone being a stranger. Namaste means that the light in me sees and honors the light within each and every one of you. When we are all in that place of peace, of oneness, we are all the same. These are words we would hear in Tao's class, and traveling through life with her, I could see how they impacted people even outside of class when practiced.

A few hours and many beautiful conversations later, Tao and I got off the train and into the waiting van that would take us to the ashram. The woman driving said that she had lived on the property for years and although she didn't personally practice yoga, she loved tending to the ashram's garden and maintaining the buildings. Tao sat up a bit brighter. She always loved hearing of women doing things that were often associated with men. As the woman continued, it was clear that she was the one in charge of the vehicles, the construction projects and the repairs. As she listened intently, I noticed that Tao was bending one knee at a time and stretching her heeled foot up toward the roof of the van. She did this a lot after traveling for a while. It was her way of sending freshly oxygenated blood back to her foot once returned to the floor. It also showed me that the trip had left her a bit tired.

As we pulled into the property, we were shown our private quarters in what looked like camp bunks. The caretaker introduced us to the woman who was coordinating the workshop.

She instantly bowed in reverence. "Tao, what an absolute honor! We cannot thank you enough for joining us this weekend. Your workshop got one of the biggest responses to our mailings and emails that we've ever received. Thank you!"

"You are so welcome. We're happy to be here with you, Dear. Look at how this property is in the middle of nature? What a beautiful setting."

"It is. My name is Coral. I'll be facilitating the workshop and helping with everything you ladies may need during your stay. We are about to begin lunch and then afterwards, before the first session of yoga, I can work with you and have the audio and mics set up." She turned to me, "Will you be handling that part?"

"Yes. Thank you so much. My name's Joanna. I'm assisting Tao." Then softly, so that Tao wouldn't hear, "Okay, so one of the few things in the entire universe that Tao doesn't like is microphones. But she totally needs one. So, let's meet a bit early and have it set up and then I can help her get it on her head."

"Does she prefer handheld or a headset?"

"Really neither because she uses her hands too much to demonstrate for the handhelds. And with headsets, the battery pack on the small of her back gets in the way of her shoulderstands and inversions." After a moment of thought, I added, "I guess the headset is the better of the two. I'll figure out the place on her waistband, maybe near her hip, that she can be heard and still be free to contort like a pretzel."

Tao was interested in a little bunny that had appeared right in front of her. The bunny kept turning its head this way and that to engage with her. They were having a full Snow White moment. But still she must've heard what Coral and I were talking about. "I don't like microphones. They get in the way of what I'm trying to show my students. But if it's a big class, I want them to be able to hear. So, I will make it work. Thank you, Coral."

"Oh Tao, thank you! For lunch, would you and Joanna like to accompany me to the dining area, or would you prefer that we have it brought to your room so that you could have privacy?"

"Oh, don't be silly. I wouldn't want anyone to go to any trouble. I don't eat very much but I'd love to see the dining area."

I put our bags in our rooms. They were right next to each other and set up identically. Quite austere with each having just a bed, some furniture and a desk with a journal and a pen. There was a simple bathroom with a shower. Notably absent was a television or a phone. In the spot where the TV would have been hung a photo of the guru that the ashram celebrated.

Walking arm in arm, Tao and I followed Coral along the path to the dining area.

Coral turned around to be sure we were keeping up and spoke to Tao. "It's so nice of you to eat in the dining hall. The people here are going to be so excited to see you. Often when Master Teachers come, they prefer to eat alone because they are approached by so many students who want to talk and ask questions."

"That's why I am here. I don't know everything but if it is something I know, I'm happy to share it. And if I don't know the answer, maybe I could find out. Questions are jewels. Each one is precious."

The dining hall looked like a converted barn. It was all wood and smelled like summer camp. In fact, the whole property really was very camp-like. Well, except when I was growing up as a sleepaway-camp-goer, they had slop that passed for food. This was different. All the produce used to make the salad was grown on site. The offerings were all vegan, organic and made by people who lived on the ashram. Great care was given to preparing and serving each dish. The communal spirit was obvious in how no one took more than what was needed and that everyone cleaned up after themselves. I had started noticing things like this more since beginning to travel with Tao. She was appalled when she'd see the very American approach to stockpiling a plate with more food than could possibly be consumed.

Coral was so engrossed in conversation with Tao that she decided to skip her next activity and join us for lunch. The food was delicious. You could taste the care that was put into it. Or at least I could since Tao hardly ate. Everyone was always baffled that she never drank water and hardly needed food. Only when distracted by great company and conversation could I subtly "trick" her into eating a few bites. So it was with pride when I saw that she had eaten a bit of vegan muffin and a few spoonfuls of the vegetable soup. Our dining began with a few people stopping at the table to greet Tao with a bow or with a handshake. Ten minutes later, she was sitting on the floor in the lotus pose fielding questions and chatting with about thirty people. Only some of them were actually registered for the workshop but details like that never mattered to her. She was in her element and thoroughly enjoying meeting people from all over the world and hearing about them.

Coral approached me looking a bit concerned. "Do you think this is too much?"

"Not at all. Tao lives for this."

"I can't believe how accessible she is. I mean we have had some presenters who're a lot less revered than Tao and will only answer questions during the sessions. She's really special."

"You have no idea. I've been following her for years and I'm blown away every time. I still hear or learn something new at each class."

"The man she's talking to right now recently lost his wife. He's been struggling. I haven't seen him smile like this since he's been here."

"That's the real gift. People will often tell her what's going on in their lives, and many times it's something tragic. She only sees the possibility that could come out of it, the light in the dark. She doesn't go into the sad with them. She invites them to the happy with her. And it's done in moments. And often without her needing to say anything."

Wondering if I lost Coral to a deep thought, I turned my head in time to see her wiping away tears. She said softly, "She's just so beautiful."

That afternoon we had an incredible workshop session. We met the group and welcomed everyone. Tao had each person share their names, where they were from and what brought them to the ashram. She delighted when she learned how many of them had traveled from all over the world and genuinely surprised that they had made the journey for her. After getting to know the students, she began with the simple question she often asked: "Would you like to do some yoga?" Simple, casual and yet it was like Picasso asking if you wanted to paint with him.

Tao began the class on the floor and had everyone connect with their breath. She loved to have students place their hands on their ribs and feel how expansive the lungs are and how much bigger our capacity for breath is. After some seated stretches and poses, she highlighted some postures and offered specific adjustments to form. Sometimes Tao would demonstrate the poses herself and other times she would use me to model as she spoke. Without words, we had begun this very intuitive and very beautiful dance of teacher/ student, mentor/mentee, guru/grasshopper, Mr. Miyagi/Daniel Son.

After leading some of her more traditional Sun Salutations, it was time for relaxation to end the class. Over the years, we had begun playing the recording of Tao's famous Savasana meditation. The sound quality of the recorded version ensured that even without a mic, everyone could hear. And it gave Tao about 12 minutes to take a breath and sit in silence. Savasana means corpse pose. It's the death of the physical practice and the chance for rebirth in mind, body and spirit. I've found in my years of teaching that this is often the hardest pose for many and the most important for all.

Gently guiding the group out of their meditative state, we closed the class by chanting "om" and making a circle holding hands. Tao loved to show how when you sent love out of your right hand and all around the circle, you felt it come all the way around and back to you. With that, our first session had ended and I could see by a glance at the faces staring back at us that Tao's magic had been received. At this stage, I always loved to see how receiving light and love could physically change someone's face. The whole group looked like they had just come out of a spa. But even more than simply looking relaxed, they looked lighter. Maybe enlightenment was just that: watching people let go enough to become light enough to be totally present. It was refreshing to be in a place where there were no phones or other distractions to rip someone back into the madness of the mind. Here, it was possible to revel in the presence—I loved seeing the students line up to hug Tao and each other.

We had another meal consisting of food grown on site and lovingly prepared. I was famished after helping Tao lead the three hour class. Tao, on the other hand, was happy to delight in the different faces from different places. Gently nagging and strategically placing vegetables I knew she'd like in front of her, I tried my best to get her to have something to eat. But she was too excited about meeting with people to humor me, except for when they mentioned that they had vegan ice cream. I immediately went to get some. Tao may have refused 90 percent of food offered but she was almost always down for some ice cream. She cleaned the bowl. While Tao enjoyed every drop of her dinner/dessert, we watched the kitchen crew seemingly turn into the construction crew as they assembled a makeshift stage.

At that point, Coral returned to let us know there would be a beautiful show with incredible musicians about an hour after dinner. We went back to our cabins where I triple-checked that Tao was up for the evening concert and when she assured me that she was, we freshened up and went back to the dining hall.

The show began and it was exactly what you'd expect if you have ever been to an ashram or on a yoga retreat. There were a number of people on stage playing interesting instruments (like a sitar) and a mixture of them singing and chanting. Occasionally I would notice a performer glance at Tao, smile, then continue. One woman, however, had a much more intense response. I saw her face when she recognized Tao, and as she continued to play her flute, tears started streaming down her face. She looked so serene, so completely at peace and yet, she clearly could not contain the emotion. The woman smiled in moments between playing, and cried as she played; all the while looking at Tao. After the show ended, a revered spiritual teacher who was also visiting, approached Tao and the two had an intense dialogue. All the while, I noticed the woman with the flute casually hanging around waiting for an opportunity to connect with Tao.

Tao was seated on a cushioned chair next to me. Her signature heels were in a basket by the door because this was a shoe-free concert. When the other teacher excused himself and walked away, the woman swept over with passion and purpose. She looked Tao in the eye and immediately bowed to kiss her feet. Tao was often embarrassed by reverence and wondered what was happening. She took the woman by the hand and had her place the flute down on the chair next to her. She held both of her hands and smiled into her face with her whole soul.

"Tao, I don't know if you remember me. I met you almost 30 years ago in New York and you changed my life. I was in a rough place when I met you."

"Oh, thank you, Dear. It's so good to see you." Tao was amazing at making people feel special even when she didn't remember them.

"You were teaching yoga and a friend brought me to your class. I was a lawyer and living a life of stress and going through a tough divorce." Her eyes filled with tears until they flooded over and spilled, once again, down her cheeks.

Tao wiped one. "You have such a beautiful smile. And your music is an extension of that smile."

"Thank you. I played for you. You changed every single part of my life. I've lived an incredible adventure these past 30 years and it was all because I met you. You saved me. Your love healed me. Your teaching inspired me. I have no idea how to thank you. I didn't even know if I would see you again and when I saw you tonight, I was so honored to play for you. I don't know how to ever thank you."

"You did it, Dear. I could say the words, but YOU did the action. You changed your life. There is no need to thank me. But if you insist, you can thank me by being happy."

As we gathered our shoes for the walk back to the room, I bent down to help Tao slide her feet into her simple black pumps. Standing, taking her arm in mine, I smiled.

In true Tao form, she looked at me and said humbly, "Wasn't it nice that that girl remembered me?"

CHAPTER SEVEN

"Be careful what you attach images to. What you see in your mind, you create in your life. Don't spend a single moment attaching a picture to something you don't want."
—*Tao Porchon-Lynch*

Still shaking, I managed to steady my hands enough to **send the text:**

Renee! It's happening. Mike just asked me to marry him on top of Vail Mountain. I'm DYING! Will u get ordained online and marry us? And shhh ... don't tell anyone. We didn't even call his parents yet.

I looked down at my phone to see if she had answered yet, hardly believing that Mommom's ring, the ring I had tried on my entire childhood, was now on my finger. I couldn't believe any of it. My whole family was waiting in the living room in the Vail rental house to continue celebrating. I had snuck upstairs for a moment. I wanted to breathe. I wanted to take it all in. I wanted to text Renee. I was dying to tell Tao but she, like I presumed was true of most magical people, was hard to reach. At one point, she had a cell phone but didn't use it to make or receive calls and eventually gave it back.

I tried so hard for so long to be a decent snowboarder, but the truth was I sucked. The first year I met Mike was the first year that we began our family trips to Colorado. My dad and stepmother took all five of their collective kids and their significant others. It was unbelievably generous. My dad had always taken us away on an annual trip but since meeting Shirlee, they started switching from the beach to the mountains. Having never been a skier, My Dude thought it would be cool if I became a boarder to "fly down the mountain together." That was his vision. The reality was that I broke my wrist on the bunny hill the second day and for the years since have simply been trying to be mediocre at it.

That morning, Mike kept insisting that he meet up with me in the afternoon to do a run together. It had already been established that Mike was part of the fast and crazy crew. The crew that went to the Back Bowls, that went down Double Blacks, and even skied and boarded after lunchtime cocktails. They compared badass experiences, accidental moguls and fun off-trail runs. Whereas my crew was comprised of my sister Jen, my stepmother Shirlee and my dad. We did the same runs over and over again very slowly and complimented each other all day on our perceived progress. The snail's pace of our group was way more my speed.

Mike would say, "Come on Babes, I'll meet you here and we'll do the last run of the day together,"

"Why though? I'm happy with Jen."

"Come on Babes. You're getting better. You can do this run now."

He was pointing animatedly to the trail map on the kitchen counter. I knew that certain parts of where he pointed looked absolutely terrifying. My dad glanced over Mike's shoulder and saw what he was suggesting. He made a face to me that looked like he had smelled something bad and I knew there was no way that he thought I was ready for that trail, but I figured it would be easier to say yes to Mike then and try to get out of it later.

When we broke for lunch, we ran into some of the family from the fast crew. They had icicles on their faces, rosy cheeks and the invigorated, excited chatter of people who'd spent the morning shredding the mountain. Our crew looked happily subdued, having taken as many bathroom breaks as ski runs.

Mike, dressed all in black helmet to boots, always looked a little too big for the sport. And also, super handsome. He let his face be scruffier in Colorado and even though it was sometimes scratchy, I was excited to see and kiss it.

He had convinced me to leave the others, assuring me that he would do a few test runs with me on an easy hill before taking me to the "scary part." True to his word, he did just that and even unstrapped his board and walked the super steep area with me. He was saying sweet things all along, but it became hard to hear over the pounding in my chest. Fears are rarely rational. I wasn't scared of heights in the way that I thought I would fall down the mountain. I was scared that I would fall OFF the mountain. That gravity would fail to exist for me as it pertained to mountains. The feeling was so deeply rooted that I convinced myself that I had perished in that exact way in a previous lifetime. By the time we got up to the run that Mike wanted us to do, we saw that it was closed. If I was even slightly Irish, I would have done a full jig with the relief that flooded through my body.

Mike went to the bathroom and I waited by the large wooden sign that held the trail map. It was the last run of the day and the light at this elevation was magnificent. The air was thinner and felt crisp in my lungs. And the sky was a combination of an electric blue against floating and fluffy white clouds. It was so beautiful. I was deep in thought feeling such gratitude for Mike "bullying" me up here. Had he not done that I would never have seen this view. I took a breath and reveled in the beauty all around me. I was scared and I did it anyway and that made me feel proud. Celebrating victories is an impactful way to attract more victory to celebrate. Align yourself with the feeling and the results flow to you. I was living out loud so much of Tao's teaching in this very moment.

There he was. My Dude. My handsome, lovey Dude. I planned to thank him for the view as he walked back to me.

"Jo. Come here."

I figured he wanted to show me (again!) the trail he wanted us to do that was closed. "It's crazy that no one else is really up here right now."

The light was getting even more beautiful, the faintest beginnings of a rainbow just off in the distance. It was breathtaking and I was taking in the mountain peaks, the snow, the sky, and now the rainbow increasing in clarity. We were ON TOP OF THE WORLD! Then I realized Mike was speaking:

"...and it isn't what I wanted to do but I know it's what you want and that's what really matters. I wanted to get you something new, from me, but I knew this is what you always wanted."

Wait, what?! I looked at Mike standing in his snow gear, holding his helmet, and suddenly he was getting shorter. I realized what was happening and I consciously thought to pause and truly take in and commit to heart and soul memory each of the subsequent moments as they unfolded. So many of the brides for whom I had done makeup had shared that their engagement was a blur. I wanted to cement the moment in my mind and heart for the rest of my life. To wrap it in a bubble forever.

"I love you Babes. I'm going to love you forever. Will you marry me?"

I looked down and my sweet, thoughtful, sexy, amazing, tall drink of water, My Dude, was on one snow-panted knee holding my Mommom's ring on top of a freaking mountain in Vail! I jumped onto that bent knee and kissed his face and kept kissing his face. In between each excited smooch, I professed my love and gratitude.

"Oh my god Dude! I love you!" Kiss. "I love you so much." Kiss. "I'm so incredibly grateful for what we've created in this relationship. I love being with you." Kiss. "I promise to be the best wife and appreciate what this is and honor it. I promise to be such an amazing mama. Oh wait!" Kiss. "Did I say yes? because I really, really mean YES!"

Standing in my black ski pants, magenta jacket and white lumberjack inspired hat, I looked at my new fiancé and felt pure joy as tears streamed down my face. Mike, far less emotional than I, would often soothe me in response to my tears. This moment, perhaps for the first time since we'd been together, was so intense that I saw he too was welling up with the beauty of it all. It was real. It was sacred. It was ours. And there was a rainbow.

I was going to marry a guy who got that Mommom's ring was the most special possible way to make me feel seen, heard, gotten. Here he was, eyes glistening, holding my face and looking right into me. We kissed and laughed and smiled all at once. It's hard to kiss and smile. Trying to kiss and smile is a good problem to have.

We reveled in the joy for a few more minutes when a couple appeared out of the lodge in perfect timing to take the requisite engagement photo for us. I then asked Mike to put Mommom's ring back into his pocket as I didn't trust myself to board with it until we got closer to the bottom. Emboldened by joy, I went faster than ever before. I felt like I was almost a real snowboarder until I caught an edge and landed flat on my back. We were so close to where the rest of the family was to meet at the gondola.

Mike flew over to the spot where I'd fallen. "You alright Babes?"

"Yeah of course. Did you see me? I was kind of amazing for a minute."

"I know. You were picking up some pretty good speed there for a bit. I thought you were going to slow down and I was cheering for you to GO GO GO. Until you bit it."

"I fell right on my butt."

"Well good thing you have a lot of cushion."

"Dude, I'm ready for the ring now before we see the rest of the fam. But love, can you propose again?"

So he did.

He knelt on the side of the mountain, as late day skiers and boarders flew past us, and asked me to marry him again. A few people noticed what was happening and cheered or clapped as they passed. None were nearly as loud though as my whole crazy family waiting at the bottom of that stretch of snow. After all the hugs, tears and well wishes, I called my mom. She was filled with love and joy and said that my dad had told her Mike asked for his blessing before the trip and that she was hoping for a call just like this.

Pure joy. And now, the plan that started as a joke in India of me telling Renee that when I was ready to get married I would love for her to perform the ceremony, was actually in motion.

I couldn't wait to get home and share the news with Tao. She had told me so many beautiful and intimate stories about her marriages. Whenever she spoke about Yvan, her first husband, a sparkle would come to her eye and she would say that he was the love of her life. You could feel the passion even 70 years later. When she spoke of her second husband, Bill, I got the sense that he was a kind man she wanted to love in the way that he loved her, but didn't. She explained Bill's courting of her as him just showing up again and again until she finally showed interest. Tao was living in New York City by the time they'd met. She was working on projects as a writer and a producer liaising between the US and India or the US and France. Her years as an actress and dancer living abroad gave her enough experience and a list of impressive contacts to help with the red tape of international production. Bill wooed Tao enough that she agreed to marry him, and in keeping with her globetrotting, the two were wed at the United Nations. It wasn't until after they were married when Tao learned they would be moving to the suburbs and would soon have full time custody of Bill's two children.

I was so curious about this phase in Tao's life because I had been with her for so long now. I had witnessed the truly unbelievable impact she had on everyone who crossed her path. Whether a complete stranger or longtime friend, she left people feeling better and more loved than when they arrived.

Just recently, I watched her working with a man who came to class for the first time. He was complaining about a shoulder that had been bothering him. When Tao put her hands on him, he was shocked by how quickly she was able to locate the exact place that was causing him pain. When he asked how she knew, she said that her ear clicked when she touched pain. I had heard her mention this for years and chalked it up to another example of Tao's otherworldly magic. Like in the movie *The Green Mile*, I assumed that she, like the character John Coffey, could energetically feel pain. But this time was different. She saw me on the next mat and had me stand up and put my ear next to hers. Petite in stature, I always marveled at her commanding presence as she taught.

She stood regally in black shiny tights with a tight black tank top. Often cold, she had a lightweight long-sleeved top over the tank. The top was blue, and magnified the sparkle in her blue eyes; the frameless glasses she wore doing nothing to dull their intensity. Her toes were impeccably polished in shiny magenta. And her nails matched as she moved her hands along the man's arm. My face was touching her lined and beautiful cheek, our ears together and nothing happening. Then, as she touched the pain spot, I heard it! There was actual clicking coming from her ear/jaw area. For so long, I thought this was something she experienced internally and so was really surprised that I could hear it on the outside. Moments like that make the magic and mystery of life accessible to us mere mortals. In this case, I got to experience a taste, a glimpse, into what it felt like to feel and process energy as Tao did.

The exception to her ability to connect with and heal those around her were her two stepchildren. One of the questions people always ask me is whether Tao had children of her own. Considering all her yoga students to be her children, she would respond by saying she had thousands. Over the years, I have come to adopt the same answer.

I found myself so curious about this and in quiet moments, would ask Tao what it was like during the phase of life where she and Bill lived with the kids in Westchester, the suburban county north of Manhattan where we both still lived.

"It was a very difficult time for me. I didn't know that they would be living with us. Bill told me only after we got married. I left New York City and an apartment that I loved to move to Hartsdale with him. I didn't know anyone and for the first time, I felt that I wasn't living in a very international place. Then when the children came to stay with us, they weren't very nice at all. They weren't nice to me, which is something I could be patient about because I wasn't their mother. But the way they treated Bill bothered me a lot. And he was such a good man. He worked with the Rotary and built bus shelters after he noticed people had been waiting in the rain for the bus. He made raised gardens so that the elderly could use them without having to bend as much. When he saw a problem, he came up with solutions. When he saw someone in need, he would always lend a hand. He even started to raise bees in our backyard. He was a good man. A solid man."

In this particular conversation, we were in my car driving home from an incredible workshop Tao had led for children in New York City. Glancing over, I noticed how serious her face had become and realized that even "lit up" beings have pain points. As we drove back to the 'burbs with the concrete jungle on our left and the East River on our right, she went into more detail.

"Their mother was very unhappy. She drank a lot and that is why they ended up coming to stay with us. In fact, whenever she would come to see them, I could tell that she had been drinking and so I would make her sandwiches. I wanted the kids to be happy in their home. We had very little money and still put what little we did have into making their rooms how they liked and buying them the clothes that they wanted. They weren't grateful and it hurt Bill very much."

"But I don't get it, Tao. I've seen you with kids and people of every age since we've been together, and EVERYONE loves you. What do you think happened?"

"Pain is a funny thing, Dear. They must have been in pain to be that angry, and that anger showed in different ways. The daughter would make fun of my accent saying that I talked funny. The son would talk back to Bill.

I tried for a long time. I've learned that when what you expect is pain, you attract more of it."

"Do you ever hear from them now?"

"No. I saw the girl recently when she came to one of my birthday dinners. Do you remember? You met her there."

I didn't remember until she mentioned it. She was at the last birthday and was sitting two tables away from me. If someone hadn't mentioned who she was, I wouldn't have known. She wasn't memorable. In a sea of people exuding joy, the only reason she stood out at all was because she hardly smiled. As I and many others spoke glowingly of Tao, she said nothing.

"Do you ever miss them?"

"Not really. I do send them love when they come into my mind. It's important to remember that no matter who you are in this world and how much good you want to do, there will be people who don't like you. And it's okay. It's simply that your energy doesn't match theirs. And that you're not meant to be together. When you notice a relationship where it seems that the universe is conspiring to keep you apart, pay attention. There is always a reason. But I have gone through life without much family and have always been blessed to create that feeling with friends, teachers and students. Your family is very special. I always tell you how I feel about your mom, the sweetest person. And your dad, he's an elegant man. But the part I love most is that you can tell that they're friends and you can tell how much they love each other. That's rare to see such closeness especially after a marriage ends."

It's true. We were lucky that our parents got along so well after being divorced for many years. It wasn't always that way, but after a few rocky years, they came back to such a solid and honest friendship. They even still wished each other a Happy Anniversary every June 15th. They celebrated and appreciated the children and family they'd created. And it was so special that my mom and Shirlee became so close. My mom would often tell my dad that if he ever did anything to screw it up that she would keep Shirlee. Our holiday tables were always loud displays of blended family love. Tao had witnessed the mayhem firsthand and I could tell that she was in awe.

"My uncle used to say if I had a problem with someone, it wasn't their fault." At the mention of her uncle, Tao's smile returned. "It was mine, because it wasn't about what the person did or didn't do. It was up to me to control my response. He taught me that forgiveness and understanding weighed a lot less to carry around than anger and negativity."

We spent the rest of the ride home talking about how amazing it was to see the children we had just taught participating so enthusiastically.

"Did you see that one boy at the end?" Tao asked.

"Which one?"

"The little boy in the blue shirt."

"Yes! He's so cute. He was hanging on your every word the whole time. I think his name is Jason."

"He asked me what I will do when I stop teaching yoga. I told him that I didn't plan on stopping. He said that was good because the world needs to feel happy. Isn't that sweet?"

"That's so cute. The kids were all between six and eight years old. I love that he's such a deep thinker at such a young age."

"I know you know because I see you work with kids all the time. You are so good at teaching children. It's important because their minds are so malleable and open to learning how anything is possible. After I told that boy that I planned to keep teaching, he asked what I will do when I die."

Wow. Out of the mouths of babes. "What did you say?" I felt like I was holding my breath. I had never really broached the subject of death with Tao. Truth be told, my reasons had much more to do with protecting my own feelings rather than hers. I knew that she would be spiritual and enlightened about it. Practically, I knew that she already had lived and contributed seven lifetimes worth. Selfishly, I just wasn't ready to imagine a world—my world—without Tao still in it.

"I told him that when I'm ready, I will dance to the next planet. That answer seemed to make sense to him because he just smiled and sat back down."

It made sense to me. And as much as I wanted to pretend otherwise, I knew that Tao wouldn't live forever. I reminded myself when such thoughts would come to mind, to revel in the gratitude of each and every moment that I was blessed to share with her. And here, in my car pulling into the driveway of the residence hotel in which Tao lived, I realized that the little boy in blue had asked the question that I hadn't had the courage to ask.

A few months after Colorado, we began the journey of planning the wedding. As my sister and I were on the phone discussing if a Halloween masquerade ball would be fun and different or hokey and distracting, I found something that made me drop the phone.

Multitasking, I was cleaning my side of our walk-in closet when I found an old box that looked worn and weathered. Interest piqued, I peeled back one of the corners that was folded inward. Immediately I found my old makeup portfolio and thought that some of the images were good and others were clearly the trying-too-hard look of a young artist. Under it was a large yellow piece of heavy-duty poster board that had been folded in thirds. I knew right away what it was but had forgotten what was on it. Years before, I had read about the power of vision boards. It was right after the rape had brought on darkness and right before Tao had returned the light. I was beginning to seek, and in one magazine I saw a mention of vision boards and thought it would be fun to do.

Forgetting that Jen was still on the phone, I unfolded the yellow poster and gasped. The entire upper right-hand corner was filled with a huge image of the Taj Mahal! I had yet to go to India and didn't even know Tao when I made this. I was living at my dad's and my only options for magazines to use were *Golf Digest* and the luxury one he liked, *Departures*. I remembered wanting something to represent exotic travel and interesting adventure and I guess that's why I chose such a big image of this majestic piece of architecture. As I looked at other aspects of the board, my sense of amazement continued. There was a picture of a sanctuary, and of a woman looking calm and peaceful and I figured that this part had predicted yoga becoming such a big part of my life and work. Moving on, in the bottom corner there was an image of a dark-haired couple taking a bubble bath together and laughing enthusiastically. It wasn't the activity that struck me—Mike is 6'4" and rarely took baths, let alone while splashing bubbles with me. It was that the man in the picture couldn't have looked more like My Dude than if I planned it! Their features, from the high cheekbones to strong jaw to soulful brown eyes, were so similar. Now in complete awe, I noticed an image of an adorable young girl jumping playfully on a bed and figured that one day he and I would have a daughter. It was all here like a roadmap of my life. There were some parts that represented family and friends and love, and then I saw the picture that made me forget about Jen and our phone call completely.

Towards the bottom of the poster, there was one more image of a little girl and in this one, she was bundled in a snowsuit ON A SNOWBOARD!

I had literally created a visual representation of the life I would create over the next five years. Suddenly Tao's message about always being aware of the thoughts you have and the power of attaching images to them became real. You literally have the power to CREATE your life. Not respond to it like many, but to dream into existence all the magic you can possibly conjure. This is what those who have achieved greatness have all figured out and what they have in common. Whether they measure their success financially, romantically, spiritually, athletically, creatively, etc., they have all seen it IN DETAIL in their mind's eye first. And the most successful at visualizing have put those images down on paper either in word or picture form.

CHAPTER EIGHT

"Children are the essence and wonder of life.
They are examples of how we are born already knowing the way."
—*Tao Porchon-Lynch*

Two lines! Two lines! I was staring into the window in my hands, staring into our future. Mike and I had been talking about starting a family since we got married at the coolest wedding ever. He, more than any guy I had dated, totally got that sports was an entrée to my heart. On our second date, he asked me to go with him to see LeBron play live in a Cavs/Nets game while they were still in New Jersey. I was cold outside of the arena because I had thought that if I wore the jacket I considered in my bedroom that it would ruin the look of my outfit. After one shiver, Mike took me into a hug to bundle in the warmth of his seasonally appropriate coat. I loved that thoughtfulness was his immediate response. I loved how he smelled so manly and I loved that his hug felt so safe.

When it was time to plan the wedding, both My Dude and I agreed that we wanted it to be a fun celebration of love; a party. We started with the idea of getting married in my dad's backyard. My dad always got choked up when I was little whenever the movie *Father of the Bride* came on. The Steve Martin classic where his "baby girl" gets married in his backyard always tugged at his heart strings. This quaint idea of an intimate homey thing turned out to be exorbitantly expensive. Bringing in tables, couches, a tent, the dance floor and fancy port-a-potties cost an arm and a leg. That was the spring of 2009. We had been engaged for a bit and the real estate bubble had popped. It impacted the economy at large and ours personally. So many of our friends had lost their jobs and shops in our community were closing. In fact, I had been looking into renting commercial space thinking that it was time for Tao to open a studio, when suddenly that became a way riskier notion. Tao and I would chat about it on the way to workshops.

"It would have to be elegant because everything you do is always so elegant, Dear."

"Thank you, Tao. It would be elegant because you would be there!"

"I know an artist who does the loveliest Indian paintings. If you want art there, that would be beautiful," she suggested.

"I love that idea. I have an idea for some clothes that we would sell too.

"If you sell clothes, you have to make some white yoga clothes too. In India, the teachers wear white and it's all so beautiful.

"We can find white outfits for you Tao."

But with the current financial climate putting the idea of a studio on hold, our conversations began to take a different path. One day we were walking arm and arm down a sidewalk to a café for lunch.

"What's happening with the space you were looking into?" she asked.

"It doesn't look like it's going to work out, Tao. My dad got nervous about the high rent when so many of the places on the same street are going out of business."

"Then it isn't the right thing. You always know when something is right because you feel it. It feels like it's already done. The idea of it gets you excited."

"I believe that, Tao. And I believe you. You always have the answers."

"You're asking good questions. You ask the questions of a seeker. That makes for an interesting life."

"You know what I got excited about?"

She paused to look at me. "What?"

"I was having a lot of fun designing clothes for the studio. What if I just did the clothes instead?"

"Voila! That sounds like a good idea." She smiled. "And I'm sure they will be elegant."

I started sketching the logo that was meant to be the logo for the studio on a napkin and realized that it would look cool on the back of tank tops. And so began the clothing line that I would start with my brother Jonny.

All of this happened over the course of our engagement. From the (almost) One Love Yoga studio (turns out that that would have been a significant law suit because of Bob Marley's estate) to Our Love Yoga clothing line, and from the backyard wedding idea to having that possibility ruled out due to cost and logistics, there was a lot of change, excitement and so much that was unknown.

I was beginning to heavily favor a masquerade ball Halloween wedding when Mike opened his *Daily News* newspaper to the sports section and turned to the spread featuring the newly built and not yet open Yankee Stadium.

"Oh Babes. Look at the stadium. It's going to be awesome."

"I'm sure. But do you think it'll be as magical as the old stadium?"

"I don't know. This one'll probably be more spread out, so I don't think it'll get as loud as the old one. So, it probably won't have the same kind of energy."

"I know. Other pitchers always talked about the old stadium feeling like the fans were closing in on them when the crowd went crazy. Anyway, Dude?"

"Yeah? Oh look, they're supposed to have a really good steak place in the outfield."

"Cool. What do you think about the Halloween wedding idea?"

"I think it could be dope. But we have to think about it. Is it a masquerade ball for the actual wedding? You're not going to want to wear a mask on your wedding day. Is that the rehearsal dinner? Would we do it as a weekend away kind of thing?"

"My dad was thinking that we probably should avoid destination."

"I get that because it definitely would make it more expensive for our friends. But it would be cool. Wow, the new stadium has party suites and areas that could accommodate up to 500 people."

"Definitely more expensive. There was a place in Saratoga that might work for a weekend. Maybe I'll look into that because then it's drivable... Five hundred people? That's a lot."

"A costume rehearsal dinner or a costume wedding could be cool. Hmm ... maybe we should get married at Yankee Stadium."

"Yeah, that would be cool. But seriously Dude."

"I'm serious Babes. They could fit our list and it definitely wouldn't be a stuffy sit-down thing. And it's the only team we have in common."

"Okay. You look into Yankee Stadium and I'll look into the Halloween one."

Four months after that conversation, we were married by Renee in the Delta 360 area of Yankee Stadium. What began with what I thought was a clever idea to get a free private tour of the stadium before it opened, resulted in Mike and me becoming the first couple to get married there. There was a film crew who wanted to use footage of our wedding for a *30 for 30* documentary on ESPN. Each episode of the sports docu-series was unique and interesting, and we thought it would be a fun thing to be featured in one. So, like good sports, we said yes!

I was walked down a baseball stadium aisle and given away by my dad, the man who grew up in the Bronx and raised my siblings and me on Yankee games. I had an ESPN battery pack taped to my inner thigh so as not to add a bulge to my dress, and an invisible mic was hidden it the cleavage dip of my halter-topped wedding gown. Mike looked so dapper in his custom-made navy and white pinstriped suit. I couldn't wait to marry him. The night was everything we wanted it to be. There were high top tables, loungey seating areas, cocktail food all night and nonstop dancing. Our ceremony had the most beautiful moments. One that would stay with me always was when we exchanged our own vows. We melded together bits from different religious and cultural ceremonies and then included our own sentiments. It was so us. My vows were lighter than most expected and Mike's were deeper than most expected.

"Thank you, Dude. For knowing when to listen to me and when to send me to Jen. Thank you for loving me as much as you love LeBron and at least tied with Kobe. Thank you for never wanting me to be less me."

"Jo, you are the light. You are my light. You bring me to that light when I am in darkness. You are my best friend."

That line of Mike's will be a touchstone for the rest of my life. Having tangoed with depression for much of his life, his acknowledgment of my ability to help him find the light in moments of darkness was the single most beautiful moment of a magically present, special day.

That night we were a mesh of limbs and joy when we finally got to bed at the Ritz Carlton in White Plains, New York. Less than five miles from our home, we decided to stay there because we wanted to continue the magic of our wedding night and feel like we were on vacation.

"Dude, I freaking love you. I'm so happy you're My Dude. I'm so happy you're My Dude forever." The chilled vodkas were still working their way through me.

"Me too Babes. That was awesome. It was so cool to see all our people in one place. Everything came out so great."

He was clearly handling his wedding liquor better than I was. "Your surr … prise … zes were sooooooooo amaaaazing. The billboard on the slideshows. I mean, the slideshows on the billboard. Whatever. Our names and picture outside the stadium. How everyone saw their own pictures and names on the screens too … everything you did was just soooooo thoughtful." I was sappy and slurry.

"It came out awesome. Everyone looked like they had such a good time. I mean, I think everyone was pretty tipsy."

Was he talking about me? "We said we wanted a party. Guess we got one. Dude, you know what I would get you, if I could get you anything, as a wedding gift?" Here I may have taken a quick trip to the toilet to return some wedding vodka.

"What?"

Replying a minute later as I returned, refreshed, from the bathroom. "Floor seats for the Lakers at the Staples Center."

"Ah, thanks Babes." He leaned in for the kind of kiss that communicates big love, all seeing love, understanding love, being understood love.

"What would you get me if you could get me anything in the world?"

He paused. It was such a pause that I was wondering if his last cocktail had just made the inevitable pass out happen quickly. Then what came out of his mouth next made me feel even more seen, more heard, more understood than I had ever thought possible from my new husband.

"I would have Tao be able to come to our wedding."

When the Yankees agreed to the terms and the date of our wedding, I was really disappointed to find that Tao was already booked under contract for a yoga appearance. So I tried to find solace in all the ways we had her energy represented. Renee wore one of Tao's hundred – year-old saris that had been fashioned into a dress, and read a poem during our ceremony that Tao had written for us. Her magic was felt throughout the event and now I had the gorgeous knowing that the man I had just married understood that that would be the only possible way to make the most special day of our lives any better.

With tears of love streaming down my cheeks and gratitude and vodka creating chills in my body, I climbed on top of my new husband and began to kiss his face, his ear, his neck.

The magic of the wedding night continued into the honeymoon and extended well into the first few years of marriage.

Keep an eye on your pinky toe or as I call it, the Lazy Little Toe. Because once the pinky toes flops out to the side, it brings the entire leg with it. Just like the roots of a tree, we draw energy upwards from the ground; from our feet. So always be mindful of how you use your feet. It communicates with your yoga lock in your navel and the energy travels from one to the other. So, watch that toe and bring it back towards your nose with energy. And just as the legs communicate with your navel, your arms are the wings of your heart. It isn't enough to breathe into your fingers. Breathe past your nails and into the universe beyond. Feel the difference. Put your arms out to the side without paying attention to your breath. Nothing. Now, really breathe. Drink in the inhale as you bring your hands to the heart center and fully exhale as you extend the arms out to the side with energy, with power, with breath. That difference. That connection of mind, body and spirit. That, is yoga.

I had sworn I was pregnant. I felt it. I had begun using an ovulation kit and when the smiley face that indicated peak time for conception coincided with Mike and I arriving at Emerson Resort & Spa in Upstate New York to celebrate of our two-year anniversary, we thought the synchronicity a sign of divinely inspired timing. I was helping put away a stray mat when I noticed that Tao was standing alone in the yoga studio. She caught my eye as I approached.

"Is something the matter, Dear?"

"Tao." I took both of her hands in mine. "I swore I was pregnant."

"Aren't you?"

Simply put.

"I really thought so. I still think so."

"So then you are," she reassured.

"I took a test two days ago and I'm not. I really thought I was though, Tao."

"You and your sweet husband are going to make such beautiful children."

"Thank you, Tao."

"Not just outer beauty because you are both so tall and striking in how you carry yourselves, but in the way you will teach your children how to be in this world. They will be lucky to have you and with that love and teaching, you can have beautiful children who will change the world. We need more happy people in this world. Children are born pure and happy and we have to encourage them all to keep that wonder. To keep that beautiful purity in how they see the world."

I couldn't resist. I couldn't hold back the desire to use some of Tao's divinity to get a crystal ball preview into my own maternity. "Do you think it will happen soon, Tao?"

"I thought you were already pregnant today when you walked in. The light around you changed colors a bit."

That afternoon I walked into town to Starbucks and called one of my best friends who I had met while working at the strip club and who lived way too far away in Texas.

"Keels. I feel like I'm crazy."

I filled her in on the whole timeline from perceived conception to the test to the conversation with Tao.

"Jo, you know what you need to do."

"I used my last test."

"Aren't you walking into town to Starbucks right now?"

"Uh huh."

"Go buy a new test dammit!"

"I said I'd wait at least until Thursday before I took another test. When they say no, it feels like a little guy comes out of that condescending little window and bitch slaps me."

"Jo. Do you think you're pregnant?"

"I do Keels."

"If you find out that you're not tomorrow, are you going to be any less bummed than if you find out today?"

"No. But I was hoping you were going to tell me to be patient and stop being a lunatic and to wait until tomorrow like I planned."

"Oh, come on. If you wanted that, you sure as shit wouldn't have called me. Now go buy the fucking test. And call me the second you find out. Or don't. But I either way, I freaking love you, homie!"

"Oh my god. I can't call you! Because if I am, I can't tell you until after I tell Mike and now if I don't, you'll read into it. So, I'm going to say now that I'm not calling you back today either way, so you don't freak out."

"I'm totally freaking out!"

"I'm freaking out!"

"I love you."

"I love you more."

About 13 minutes later, I was standing in the bathroom holding the test and staring at the two lines. The second line was faint, but it was definitely there. Undeniably there. I was shaking. I suddenly felt like there was so much to do and also nothing to do. I wanted to tell everyone and yet I couldn't tell anyone. I wanted to share the news with My Dude, but he was at work. Ultimately, I wanted certainty. Certainty as it pertained to a miracle. And that desire dictated my first step.

After three rings, two rounds of being put on hold and a bit of Muzak later, I was connected with the nurse who worked with my OB/GYN. I filled her in. "So, can I please come in for a blood test? Because, no pressure in finding time to squeeze me in ... but I may not breathe until you do. I so need a test to confirm it."

The nurse who'd known me for years just chuckled and told me to hang up and come right in. Already in the car, I buckled my seatbelt, put the gear in reverse and cried my way to confirmation of our miracle. On the way to the office, I knew in my heart that this was it. Tao had seen the color change around me.

Over the next nine months, I marveled, with awe, at what the female body could do. I held my belly as I felt the first movements. I would rub my hands together and create heat between them. Once warmed up, I would put them on the bump and chant the sound of "om." Babies feel vibration before they even hear sound, so this was a touchstone of connection between us. Mike and I would listen to the same mantra each night in bed. I would take his hand and cover it with my own. And even though many of the nights he did this while watching the Lakers on his iPad, I knew that this ritual was creating a loving bond of our soon to be family every night.

As I and my belly grew bigger and bigger, we would wonder what each pokey body part was as the baby would move in waves in utero. I continued to teach and practice and to run the clothing business all throughout my pregnancy. My body responded differently to yoga and most people expected that I would modify how I used this new shape ... most people, except for Tao. In classes and workshops, she would have me demonstrate exactly as I would prior to conceiving. At our weekend in Kripalu when I was over seven months pregnant, the students looked aghast at me in a very pregnant headstand. Tao simply explained to them that when you are in tune with your body, you understood how to use it. I made it clear that we didn't recommend pregnant headstands as a rule but that the breath was our teacher and if you moved beyond it, that was your indicator that you'd gone too far.

The clothing line was such a labor of love. I loved designing the images and seeing them come to life. I loved working with my brother. He was so good at the parts of business I didn't enjoy. He was like a living spreadsheet. I really loved meeting with vendors and landing the deals and he expertly filled the orders. The first time Equinox placed an order for over twenty locations, I jumped into Jonny's arms in the warehouse. After having a few more major gyms, yoga studios and stores sign up to carry us, it started to feel like we were taking off. We made custom outfits for Tao because no one else seemed to want unforgiving, tight white pants. She wore the clothes beautifully as she taught and traveled. It was so exciting when we were featured in photo shoots, magazines, on celebrities, etc. Gabby Bernstein, who had already become such a beautiful example of a modern-day spiritual icon, chose Our Love Yoga as the brand she wanted to curate for a boutique website. It looked like everything was coming up roses, except our profits.

Jonny's wife Beth was also pregnant. He and I realized that the cash cycle of our business would not work for our new families. The company was so inventory-laden that by the time we were paid for one job, we had already used that money to produce the next. Our model wasn't profitable. And some of our best-selling items were starting to get copied by other brands, which was something that always annoyed Jonny. Whereas I thought that his practicality was getting the better of him. I thought it meant that we had ideas worth stealing. So much of life is in how we choose to see it. Despite our differing ways of seeing the world, my brother and I agreed that it was time to look for other options. We couldn't each start our families while working full time in the hopes of someday becoming profitable, so we decided that it was time to sell the business.

I was due on May 15th, 2012. That year, Mother's Day fell on May 13th. I swore I was going to go into labor that day as I loved the numbers one and three and was about to become a mom. What better day than on a holiday celebrating moms? As Tao considered all of her students to be her children, I made it a ritual to go to her classes or have lunch with her on Mother's Day. Usually my mom came with me and it was extra special. Given that I could pop in at any moment, that year Mike decided to come to class too. In fact, we were at the point in pregnancy where my feet were a distant memory and if something dropped on the floor, it was gone forever. Mike and I had already decided that if the baby was a girl, we would name her Natasha Tao. I thought it would be cool if her nickname was Nataraj, which is the Sanskrit word for "Great Dancer" pose.

When we got to class, I was doubly excited to see Renee there and felt the love when I took a photo with her and Tao each placing one hand on my now enormous belly. That day, the mayor of White Plains came to the studio to surprise Tao with the distinction of having May 13th forever be known as "Tao Porchon-Lynch Day." Now I was certain our miracle would come. The 13th and Tao day—it felt all too auspicious. As we settled in for the session, my mat was placed behind Tao's to assist her without getting in her way. Mike had his mat next to mine and his camera at the ready. He loved Tao and never stopped staring in awe as she did her signature arm balances and advanced postures. This day was no exception. She began her class as she always did with seated work. As she had us get to our feet, the first pose she decided to teach was Nataraj, and the only person she decided to assist in it was Mike. I saw this and through tear-filled eyes, mouthed to him *THAT IS THE POSE! THAT'S NATARAJ.*

I should've known in that moment that we would have a girl. She came on her due date two days later.

A few months later, we celebrated Tao's 94th birthday and I read this poem aloud with Natasha Tao slung to me:

When I was born, Mommy & Daddy thought long and hard of whom they hoped I would emulate.
They really believed I would be blessed or marred, that the name shouldn't be left to fate.
So Mommy talked and Daddy listened, which is often how it goes.
They chose wisely and the eyes did glisten as Mommy's tears began to flow.
They knew I'd be a special one, filled with peace, light and love.
That I'd always be ready for any fun with a sparkle that was sent from above.
Both wanted me to reach great heights and to never give in to fear.
To achieve any goal I set in my sights and to doubts turn a deaf ear.
But who could embody all of these traits, to be kind, powerful and bold?
Who's able to take on all that awaits with a peaceful presence to behold?
Of course the answer we all know is as beautiful as any corsage.
The woman who predicted that Mike was for Jo would be the inspiration for Nataraj.
My Mommy is unusual I'm told, and it's because someone showed her how to spread love and never grow old, we're so grateful to our special Tao.
At 94, you have achieved so much; a guru, a master, a light.
So many people you have touched, you're a star that shines so bright.
At three months old, I'm a lucky girl and I know this to be true,
Mommy and Daddy named me Natasha Tao so that I can be just like you.

CHAPTER NINE

"Just look at the trees. They lose their leaves, but they aren't dead.
They are rejuvenating themselves. When it looks like nothing is hap-
pening that is when everything is happening. And just like the trees,
we recycle ourselves with each new day with each new breath."

—Tao Porchon-Lynch

The Native Americans would go outside and wrap their arms around trees. They
knew that if they turned to nature, they could find the answers. When they hugged
the trunks, they could feel the energy that connects us all rising like smoke from the
ground. People may think I'm mad, but I love hugging trees. And watching animals.
And marveling at the ocean. They are beautiful examples of the power that lies in
each and every one of us. So, when you do tree pose, don't simply put one sole of the foot
against the other inner thigh. There is no energy there. No life. It brings the bent knee
down like a weeping willow. And with that, you will feel a heaviness. We want to feel
the energy of the ages rising through our whole body: from the roots of our feet through
the trunk as it passes through each chakra and out of the branches of our arms and
past the leaves of our fingertips. That is the life force, or prana, moving within us. So,
as you do tree pose, place the ball of the foot against the opposite inner thigh and leave
the heel apart. Yes, yes. Now you are doing it. Beautiful.

Tao's simple cueing, married with illustrative language and completed
with loving assurances of progress made the students feel guided, supported
and loved. People drove (and sometimes flew) from all over the country (and
the world) to attend her weekly Sunday classes. The recognition by *The
Guinness Book of Records* as the "World's Oldest Yoga Teacher" was really having an impact. News stations, television shows and magazines were constantly
calling to invite Tao to be a guest. Having not watched television or read
magazines regularly, she typically had no idea who the people were or why

they wanted to connect with her. But nevertheless, she patiently answered every question and gave of herself fully to each appearance. Some opportunities were direct hits, others were strange bedfellows.

For example, when the Panel for Peace gathered in New Jersey in 2011, it made complete sense for Tao to be on the same stage as Deepak Chopra and His Holiness the Dalai Lama. In fact, there was a beautiful photo from that event that showed the Dalai Lama looking at Tao the way most people looked at him. It was as if two light seekers connected and instantly, wordlessly, acknowledged being on the same path of peace, of love. When I asked her what she felt when she was with the Dalai Lama, she said she felt the pure energy of youthful happiness and exuberance of presence when they held hands. Around that time, fellow ageless goddess Jane Fonda, became enamored of Tao and flew her out to California to film a yoga video. Tao saw the good in it all and viewed everything she did as a chance to have an adventure and to spread peace. She summed things up so simply, focusing on energy more than fame; on love more than popularity, and on impact more than income.

Once on a family ski trip to Colorado, Natasha Tao was taking a break from her baby ski school and having a nap and lunch with me at our rental house. When I fed her, she pointed to the TV. Not knowing the channels in Vail, I found the remote and simply pressed the power button. As the screen came to life, I realized *The Steve Harvey Show* was on. "Tashi" kept pointing to the screen with excitement that was hard for her to contain until finally she pushed away the spoonful of sweet potato I was trying to feed her. When I turned to see what had piqued her interest, I realized that she wasn't saying "-to" for "potato." She had been saying "Tao." There she was, our girl, in her leggings and high heels, demonstrating postures gracefully and beautifully. Steve Harvey was hardly able to contain his utter amazement. As for Tashi, it seemed she was just happy to see her Tao on our family trip.

About a year and many national and international appearances later, Tao and her dance partner went on *America's Got Talent*. Before they performed, they showed some B-reel of a backstage interview with Tao and Vard. He shared the story about how they met and how they had been dancing together ever since. When they came out onto the stage, the judges were happily in shock to learn that at 97, Tao was dancing with a partner who was 27. They invited them to begin. At the start of the number, Tao and Vard began slowly and the audience and judges likely thought they'd be watching the performance of a cute old woman. Suddenly, the record scratched and the music changed to a Pit Bull song. They strutted their stuff across that entire stage. Vard flung her through the air and spun her all around. It was energetic and fun and completely uplifting. Even Howard Stern had to marvel in awe when they were done. He mentioned how Tao could inspire his parents who were also in their 90s to perhaps get off the couch.

When I asked Tao about the show later that week, she simply said she had waited a long time to do one dance and that the venue was very cold. "We made it fun. But it was freezing in that green room. And I'm not exactly sure what they do on that show. They want me to come back, but I think that was enough."

I was overjoyed. "Tao, you're a Rockstar! Everyone wants a piece of your wisdom, your vitality, your YOU-ness." We were in the car driving upstate to a yoga center about an hour away. It was nice to have this time alone together. Now, with my life as a mom and Tao being in more and more demand, I reveled in these quiet moments when we could really connect before and after our workshops.

"I don't know about a rockstar, but truly, everyone has been so sweet to me. What is happening with you? And that special little girl of yours?"

"Everything's amazing. I love being a mama. She's smart and funny and stubborn and brave."

"She is already doing beautiful yoga. I saw that when you brought her to my party. She sat right next to my chair and started imitating me on the dance floor, and that's when I knew this little girl can do anything. In fact, you will not be able to tell her no. You can see it in her eyes. Once she makes up her mind to do something, she will. Nothing will stop her."

"Tao, you're spot on about that. She has the strongest will. It's true that you should be mindful when naming a baby after someone because you will transfer some of the energetic qualities. So, I can now say that I fully believe that, and that I know what you must have been like when you were a toddler."

She let out a small giggle that crinkled her sparkly eyes and lit up her face with joy. "Oh, I was a handful, I'm sure. I had very definite ideas from the time I was a little girl." Her face was still exuding joy but suddenly became more serious. "But I had my uncle and he understood me. And she has you, and your sweet husband. And you will understand her. And that will give her permission to go out in the world and do whatever is in her heart."

"Thank you, Tao. I have some business ideas and retreats for underserved teens that I want to lead. There's so much that I want to do and yet, I'm also loving simply teaching and focusing on being a mom."

"Dear, I want you to make a lot of money."

This was one of the first times in all my years with Tao that I was completely taken aback by something she had said. Sure, I'd marveled when she shared her incredible history and I'd teared up when she poetically expressed her views of the universe. But this sentence was so surprising that it caught me off guard. And she said it with such conviction of voice and intensity of gaze. "Tao, I think in all of our conversations, this may be the most surprising advice I've ever gotten from you."

"I've never been good at the money part of things. I just did everything I believed in and knew that it would somehow work out."

"That, I get."

"Money is energy. It's inherently nothing. It's what you do with it. We need more of the good people to have the money and to use it to change the world."

"You're absolutely right."

"I've sometimes wondered if I had been better with the money part if I could've spread this message of peace and possibility even farther. So, go out and make a lot of money. And then use that money to change the world."

And just like that, I had my marching orders. I never had given it much thought before this conversation, but in that moment I realized that I had subconsciously capped my earning potential thinking that spirituality and financial abundance were somehow mutually exclusive. "Well, Tao. You never cease to amaze me. I learn something from you every time we're together and today is no exception. I guess coming from someone who's found her celebrity in her 90s, I should no longer be shockable. But thank you, Tao. Things haven't been exactly easy financially lately. I feel the weight of the financial burden that Mike is carrying on his shoulders. I needed this talk more than I'd even realized."

"Mike is a sweet young man. And he has a quiet strength so don't worry too much about his burden. But do go after your dreams. And don't apologize for the success you will find. Too often, especially with women, we don't celebrate the important things we do. And you have that little girl watching everything you do so do it with love and power. And let people celebrate the success you will have. You are married to a man secure enough to watch you fly with pleasure. So do it. Fly."

When we arrived at the workshop to lead our class, I silently reflected on how my lesson of the day was already delivered. In the opening meditation, when everyone had their eyes closed, I glanced over at Tao. I always sat slightly behind her when I assisted, wanting to leave the full light and focus on her. I noticed, even in profile, that Tao was changing and starting to look older. I recognized what a silly sentiment that was to have about someone in her late 90s. She was beginning to be a little less steady in her signature heels. I would see her defer to me to demonstrate things that she used to insist on doing herself. There was a shift. The thought filled me simultaneously with melancholy and with gratitude. I closed my eyes and breathed a wordless thank you to the universe that had determined our friendship was to be a decades-long reality and then brought my focus back to the class.

About an hour later, she was describing a way to get into a pretty advanced arm balance posture. It was a pose that I had yet to achieve. Tao, having taught it at our weekly class that Sunday, knew that I wasn't able to do it. Yet, with a twinkle in her eye, she declared that I would be demonstrating the pose.

"I will?"

"Yes. You will."

And I did. The magic of Tao is that her belief in you can be enough for you in the moments when your own wavers. She subtly stepped on the outside edge of my foot to have me feel how grounded it needed to be. She verbally cued what to do with each breath and each movement of the arms until before I knew it, I was balanced with one arm and one leg on the ground and the other leg stretched over my head with the other arm. I felt strong and empowered like I could do great things. Tao's guidance and cueing were magical combinations; even more important than the fact that I had done the pose for the first time through demonstrating it, the class was inspired to try it too. I shared that I had never before gotten it and that the energy of the grounding back foot was the key. Before long, many of the students were stretching their legs over their heads. Tao's face alit with joy. These were her favorite moments. The moments of transformation as she watched people do what they didn't know they could.

CHAPTER TEN

"Procrastination is the only sin. Whatever is in your heart, do it. And do it today. For tomorrow never comes. One minute after midnight is already today again. So, don't just think about, be about it. And don't just be about it, go out and DO IT."

—*Tao Porchon-Lynch*

Some days I miss Mommom so much that the weight of her absence feels like a presence in my chest. Today was one of those days. I had woken up to the screaming cry of my now four-year-old Natasha. Her favorite pink and purple blanket had fallen out of her bed and apparently, that was ruining her life. I got her and brought her into our bed and began the snuggle fest that was usually my favorite part of the day. But today was different. I couldn't summon my usual early morning joy. I had made a practice of beginning each day with three gratitudes and focusing on them enough to feel them in my mind and body. Today, I went through the motions but the warmth that typically flooded my body was instead puddling at the surface.

I knew it wasn't just one thing. It was all the things. Tao had always taught to pile the good things and not the bad. Because when you notice a pattern and then talk about that pattern, you invite it to continue and to increase in size. If I started to mentally rattle off all the things that were causing me angst, I'd only attract more of the same. In theory, the brilliance of that message was clear. In practice, I was struggling and sometimes more than others.

About a month before it came out that there was an old business loan that Mike had taken out without telling me. All the financial stress I had seen in him had finally made sense. I had always thought that we were doing fine and wondered why he had this weight. We would talk about it, but something felt off. There was this feeling that his worry was less about planning for our future and more about dreading something in our present. Now that the debt had come to the surface things suddenly made sense. As much as I tried to reassure him, it didn't seem to work. What is hidden in the dark always comes to the light. I was so disappointed by this point in our relationship, in our MARRIAGE, that he didn't realize what we had. Didn't he know that I'd support him through anything? We could overcome any hurdle as long as it was together. But no! He did that very male thing of trying to sweep it under the rug and handle it himself until the pile became so big that the rug and the room around it all crumbled. What was once a small issue that could have been solved with a little bit of help or perhaps a loan from family was now an issue that could result in foreclosure on our home and possible bankruptcy.

I was pissed.

And sad.

Not knowing any of this, we had been trying to get pregnant for over a year. I knew in my heart that we were meant to have more children and that Tashi was going to have a sibling. But test after test telling me otherwise was beginning to dull the shine on my belief. I would meditate on the idea of telling Mike that I was finally pregnant and visualize myself snugly holding our new baby to my chest. All along, Mike had been watching my ovulation tests and charting my cycle with me. When I asked him why he was doing this when he was clearly under some heavy burden—which later was revealed to be his big secret—he answered simply that he didn't think we could afford to wait because of my age.

None of this felt good as I laid in bed next to my husband. I knew the stress wouldn't do anything to help bring about a speedier solution, so I had taken to compartmentalizing. When I was with Natasha, I was in full mama mode. When I was teaching or assisting Tao, I was hyper aware of being as helpful and impactful as possible. And when I was alone with Mike, I was trying my hardest to connect with him and to release the anger I was feeling about him pulling away from me; it was like he was keeping me in the dark about something. I knew that allowing seepage of negativity from one area into the other would only contaminate the good, but this mindset struggle was becoming a full-time dialogue in my head.

When my phone buzzed, I glanced at the text to see that it was a message about Tao. Never from Tao since she still didn't text or have a phone, but about Tao. Two days before, she had broken her wrist when a Russian television crew was interviewing her and wanted B-roll for the piece. They had her doing her signature peacock pose again and again as they adjusted the lighting and the framing of their shot. Peacock is like a plank (or a push up position) except the feet are elevated off the ground. On the final time, her wrist collapsed under her weight and broke. She was in the hospital for the day and now back at her home. Those of us closest to her had arranged care in a subtle enough way that the stubbornly independent Tao would accept. So I texted back that Natasha and I were free to bring her lunch and have a quick visit.

It was then that I saw the date at the top of the phone and realized why I had been feeling so emotionally fragile. It was Mommom's birthday. With tears streaming down my face, I switched Natasha to my outside arm so that I could lean in to be spooned by Mike.

He stirred. "What's the matter, Babes?"

I sniffled and took his big arm and wrapped it around Tashi, the pink and purple blanket and me.

"Are you crying?"

"Yes."

He sat upright. "What's up?"

"I woke up feeling so off. Then I saw my phone and saw that it's Mommom's birthday."

"But why are you crying? Usually you're happy to think about Mommom. And then you see a ladybug and it's all good. Why don't you show Tashi pictures of her or something?"

"So much is going to shit right now . . . and I just miss her so much." What had started as a few tears became a full-on cry fest. Tash, who had fallen back asleep in my arms, was beginning to stir.

"I know it's a lot, Babes. It's going to all work out though. We'll figure it out. And we'll figure it out together. I'm sorry that it's adding extra stress to you. Especially now that we're trying to get pregnant."

"I'm worried about Tao." I resented even saying that out loud and didn't realize how true it was until I had said the words.

That stopped him. He is so much more practical than I and he has the ability to reduce big overarching themes into simple thoughts. He put his head back comfortably on the pillow and I felt him kiss my hair.

"Babes. Tao's almost 100. And she's the strongest person you know. I know it's going to be tough for you when the day comes that she's not here anymore, but you have to know whenever that happens that she's had some run."

"I know."

"And that you've been so lucky to have this special friendship with her for all these years."

"I know. It feels so big right now. All of it."

"I get it. And you know whenever that time comes, it'll be on Tao's terms. And I'll be here with you and for you. Because I said Tao is the strongest person you know. But YOU are the strongest person I know. And also the softest."

With the last line, he was squeezing more than a handful of my butt. It had the desired effect of making me laugh and shifting my focus away from the heavy thoughts in my head. With Tashi in bed with us, a quick laugh was the best he could hope for.

The next few months became a season of healing. Tao's wrist was getting stronger and although her signature peacock pose became a thing of the past, she was able to teach and make appearances and continue her dance lessons.

Mike and I were close to solving the big issue resulting from the loan. With the help from my dad and some miracles of timing and connection, it looked like we would be able to resolve this without negatively impacting our credit or our future. I silently prayed that the bigger issue, the foundational cracks of my trust, would also heal. But at least it had begun. As scary as some of the talks had gotten, I noticed he was lighter. When carrying a secret that could hurt his family, the weight of it showed in different ways. For Mike, I would sometimes notice that his smile didn't reach his eyes or that in a happy family moment, he wasn't really there even when he was. In the past few months, that had shifted. He seemed more present and more attentive. I believed that we would get through it and I prayed that he would know that what we had was magic. That didn't mean a life without problems. What it meant was that problems were solved faster, easier and with more love when we did it together.

As for the baby journey, that was a different story. I watched my family members and friends as they announced their pregnancies. I celebrated each one showing up to the showers, sprinkles, sip 'n sees; anything and everything baby related. When manifesting anything in life, seeing someone else have it first should merely serve as a reminder of the possibility. It is when people think that that car "took my spot" that they invite a scarcity mindset. But abundance mindset will say instead "that was their spot and good for them." And "thank you for the one coming for me." In fact, one of my favorite ways to teach the four steps to manifesting is so well illustrated with that parking scenario. It works like this:

Step 1: Ask for what you want and BE SPECIFIC. In New York City, for example, I would ask for a spot that was legal, safe, free and immediately available right by my location.

Step 2: Have absolute faith that this will happen. In a sea of Manhattan street signs instructing you not to park on a day that ends in Y or if your mom is wearing a yellow dress or if your car has wheels, the magic is in seeing the spot and absolutely expecting it.

Step 3: Releasing. Often the hardest step for most, is letting go of control of the how, what and why. Enjoying the unfolding is a step that trips up many. It leads to thinking that the other guy got "your spot" or to fixating on which street to turn on next. True release comes with a feeling of peace, of happy expectation.

Step 4: Gratitude. Say thank you when you see your spot, as you pull into it and as you step out of the car. Your wish was granted. Your prayer was answered. The parking space example may seem silly but it's small and practical enough that it serves as a fantastic way to practice this process. And this process works on everything. The gratitude step is what keeps the conversation with the universe in flow and seamlessly transitions into the next Step 1.

This is what I have practiced. For years.

The last round of hormones injected into my butt and belly were taking a toll on me. Feeling bloated and inflamed, hopeful and worried and happy and sad, I was losing control of my spiritual and physiological connection. I turned to Tao and to meditation even more. I would so clearly visualize seeing the test that confirmed I was pregnant and joyfully telling Mike. I would see our new baby and fantasize about Natasha meeting her new brother or sister for the first time. But my mindset work was becoming maniacal and obsessive and Step 3 was proving to be a challenge.

After three rounds of IUI had failed, we realized that the "turkey baster" Intrauterine Insemination method of fertility help wasn't working. The doctor met with the two of us right before I was to turn 40 and said that he strongly recommended we move on to IVF. In vitro fertilization, while not perfect, would increase the odds of conception from about 30 percent to 50 percent. He gave us the stats calmly, advised professionally and then left Mike and me in the room to chat about it ourselves.

"What are you thinking, Jo? I know you were never really into the idea of doing IVF."

"I know. I always thought if it was meant to be, it would happen and if it didn't, we would be happy and grateful that we already have a healthy and amazing kid."

"Is that what you're feeling now?"

"I don't know Dude." And it all unleashed. Emotions I thought to be contained and tears that I thought already shed flew out of me in wracking sobs. With mascara mixing with tears causing black wet rivers down my cheek, I continued. "I can't even picture Tash going through life without siblings. Look how close I am to Jonny and Jen. And look at you with Kris. Imagine if we didn't have them?"

"I know Babes. But she has her cousins, and she sees them all the time and she loves them so much. It's almost the same."

"She said to me yesterday she wants a baby that lives with us like all her cousins have. She asked if I could 'get us a baby.' Then I heard her ask the magical tree I painted in her room to put a baby in Mommy's belly. It broke my entire heart."

"Jo, Tash is amazing. If we have a baby, she is going to be such an awesome sister. But if we don't, she will still be funny and smart and a stubborn pain in the ass and all the things we already know her to be."

"What do you want to do?" I asked, exhausted.

"I think we should do it. I pay for the expensive health insurance at work and it covers one round of IVF. I say let's go for it. Your butt already looks like a pin cushion and your body has been through so much. I know IVF will be even more, but it isn't that big of a jump from what you've already been doing with IUI and it'll make the outcome of getting you pregnant so much more likely. I say 'fuck it.' Let's have our baby."

He made me laugh, cry and snort on that one. "So that's the deep thought ... fuck it, let's have a baby?"

"Yeah. You want to?"

"Okay. Let's do it. Fuck it."

The doctor came back in and we made a plan. The clinic closed for much of December so we would start the process in January. This gave us a month for clarity, reset and meditation. It also gave me the green light to relax and celebrate turning 40.

Anyone who experiences a fertility journey, experiences it differently as it's a deeply individual and personal event. We committed to one round of IVF and were literally putting all my now 40-year-old eggs in that one basket. Along the way, we had conversations we never imagined having such as about filling out papers stating that should one of us die, the other one could or could not choose to use the frozen eggs. This chat turned out to be moot as none of our fertilized embryos were deemed worthy of being frozen. When the day came to implant, we went from having 11 that fertilized to having two and a half viable candidates. They rate them with letters, and we had no straight A students. Initially the doctor suggested putting three in and seeing what happened. We decided to go with two: the B and the B-. By the time I was wheeled into the operating room, they said that the B – was getting better and better and that if it were a horse race, that's the one they'd place their bet on. I listened to one of Tao's guided meditations as the anesthesia began to take me.

Weeks later, I was sitting up in bed watching Mike sleep. You can take a pregnancy test on the first day of what would be a missed period. I kept staring at my clock wondering if three AM counted as the next day or if I must fall asleep and wake up again for it to really be morning. Two days before, I had asked Tao to put her hands on my belly and to connect with the miracle of our new baby. Her words kept replaying in my mind.

"You are going to have a little boy this time. And that handsome husband of yours will have so much fun playing with him."

I told myself that to be reminded of our miracle was all I needed. The why behind the what. All of the tears, the needles, the praying. It was all for this. A baby that would complete our family. A sibling for Natasha.

At 5:01, I congratulated myself on having such incredible restraint and tiptoed to the bathroom. Not wanting to mess around with whether the second line was dark enough to count, I paid the extra $7 to get the test that said PREGNANT or NOT PREGNANT.

I peed.

I prayed.

I waited.

The timer on my phone chimed and I took a breath. Turning on the iPhone flashlight, I sighed as I took the test off the side of the sink. Shining the light on it I saw PREGNANT and sank to the bathmat crying in gratitude. I talked to the baby and welcomed him or her to our family. I sat there for a few minutes breathing in the magic of a miracle manifested before waking up Mike.

Pretending I couldn't read what the screen said, I had him turn on a light and look. With one eye opened, he saw the word and hugged me into him. In all the months and years of trying, one of the fantasies that kept me going was the one where I would think of creative ways to break the news to him.

This way was none of them. But it was sweet and sacred and ours.

Our lives have seasons. And as Tao teaches with nature, we can learn and gain something from each of them. The season of struggle was a planting season and we were now harvesting. With the loan issue complete, we were starting anew. We sold our apartment and were ready to move on. Instead of focusing on how costly this life lesson had been, we were excited to have a clean slate and a new beginning. I was letting go of the hurt from the secret itself and reconnecting with Mike with special date nights. Because when making a baby, the baby making part of it can turn into more science than romance and as my high school chemistry teacher would say to my mom during conferences, I was not scientifically inclined. Now, with the news of our second baby, everything was seeming to go in a lit-up direction. Tao no longer wore a brace on her wrist and her teaching and workshops were as busy as ever.

One morning, a few weeks later, my brother called to see if I could go to a school event the next day for my nephew, Jax. He and his wife were both working and Jax asked if Tash and Aunt Jo Jo could go instead. These were the moments where I was so grateful not to be working a traditional nine to five job. I loved the freedom of being able to say yes and to be there for the kids whenever they wanted or needed me. For instance, I had happily waited at the stop when each of my nieces and nephews got off the bus on their first day of kindergarten. I went to all their shows, plays, games and graduations. Which meant bringing Natasha to Jax's family lunch was right in my wheelhouse.

Still in the "secret" phase of pregnancy, I was feeling good but tired. As a result of the hormones and injections, even though we weren't making it public knowledge yet, I was showing within five minutes of that positive pregnancy test. And I was constantly thirsty. When we got to the school, Natasha instantly ditched me to find her cousin/best friend/"twin" Jax. The two were seven months apart and inseparable. Their love and friendship was ridiculously cute. I loved watching a mini me and a mini my brother and the silly games they would create just as we had.

Then I walked to the refreshment table to get water and looked up right into his face.

The rapist.

My breath caught in my throat and my hand instinctively went to my developing bump. The mama bear urge to protect the cub starts way before the cub enters the physical world. I made a sound that was a mix between a cough, hiccup and gurgle. It was something guttural that I didn't consciously release. The rapist didn't even notice. Immersed in conversation with a few moms, he stood there; a smiley dad in the suburbs.

He looked a bit older and softer, but his face was basically the same. His thick eyebrows added an intensity to his look, like one of the Angry Birds. He had tattoos down one of his arms and cradled in it was a little girl. She was babbling as she clutched a doll tightly to her chest. It was strange to reconcile seeing the face from my college nightmares in such an innocuous situation holding an innocent baby. I thought I was going to be sick.

I knew I was going to be sick.

I checked on Natasha and Jax and saw that were totally engrossed in a game with some of his classmates. I slunk off to the bathroom without anyone noticing. Standing over the small elementary school toilet sure that I would vomit, I waited. When nothing happened a few minutes later, I went to the sink and scooped some of the cold water into my mouth. Though not warm in the building, I suddenly felt flushed. I wet a paper towel and used it to cool the back of my neck. I looked in the mirror and silently reminded myself: *I'm a different person from the girl he raped. A mom, a yogi, a wife, a grown-up. And happy. I am a spiritual badass and seeing him can't negate any of that.*

But the pep talk wasn't working, so I did the only thing I could think of; I texted Jen and Mike.

Me: Omg Jen, I don't know what to do.

Jen: Aren't you at Jax's school today?

Me: Yes. The rapist is here

Jen: WHAT? Get out. I want to kill him. Go! Leave.

Me: No. I'm here for Jax. I'm not letting him make me leave.

Jen: Did he see you?

Me: I don't think so.

Jen: OK. Call me if you need me and if you don't feel okay, LEAVE. I love you.

Me: Love you

Jen: Remember who you are, Jo.

Me: Dude, I'm at Jax's school and the fucking guy is here. The rapist.

Mike: Are you serious? Are you okay?

> Me: Not really. I feel like I'm going to throw up.
>
> Mike: Did he see you?
>
> Me: I don't know. I saw him and thought I was going to puke
> and came to the bathroom to breathe and text you.
>
> Mike: Do you want to leave?
>
> Me: Yes, but I'm not going to. I came for Jax and I'm not letting
> that mother fucker get to me.
>
> Mike: Are you sure?
>
> Me: No. But thank you.
>
> Mike: I love you Babes. I'm sorry. Call me if you need me.

Deep breath. Inhale light, exhale love. I got this. I checked my reflection to make sure I wasn't wearing the negativity on my face because Natasha, much like Tao, was able to read me in a moment. Confident that my appearance didn't bely what I was feeling inside, I left the bathroom.

I wanted to avert my gaze, to look anywhere else except at him, but I couldn't. I kept resetting to focus on Jax and Tash and how much fun they were having, but it didn't last. Like the predator tracking its prey or the prey keenly aware of the predator, I couldn't help but stare. I felt such conflicting emotions and wasn't sure how to reconcile them. His daughter was adorable and typically I'd swoon over any little kid. But he gets to be her dad? A guy who raped me, stole from our house, took my mom's ring from her DEAD FIANCÉ! How did he end up a dad to this cute little girl? I also knew he had to have more kids around Jax's age to even be at this event.

The teachers asked the parents and grown-up guests to help serve the pizza and drinks. Not often allowed juice, Tash was living her best life because I distractingly said yes to lemonade. She probably could've asked for the keys to my car and in my state of mind then, she would've been the first kid driving before the age of six. They cut each slice of pizza in half to serve the young kids. With Jax, this was always an exercise in futility as he ate three before most kids were served their first. As usual, Natasha was telling him that she didn't like pizza. Watching her as she ate the pizza, I realized my silly, normal musings about kids were saving me. They were keeping my feet rooted to the ground when I felt shiftless. Their giggles were bringing me back as I mentally floated backward. And I realized I still hadn't let go of my bump. Being pregnant means being vulnerable.

In that state of heightened awareness, I couldn't visualize ninja kicks to his testicles or other revenge fantasies. Instead, it prompted me to go deeper. After all, I didn't need revenge. His rape had led to all the greatest gifts in my life: the Italy trip, the semester abroad, the nightclubs, Tao, India, Mike, my family. If one thing had changed, the ripple effect would have changed all things. I realized with ever increasing clarity that the gratitude I had felt for the trauma was now being given an opportunity to shift into forgiveness of the abuser.

But not before I said what I needed to say.

I saw my moment. He was standing alone, the kids occupied in a group activity. I walked over to his general vicinity and stood near him without being too close. It had the intended effect. He glanced up a few times and I noted that he was looking at me, trying to place me. I let that happen a few times until the last time when he looked up and smiled.

I felt myself respond physically. My hands were starting to sweat and feel cold at the same time. I was shaking. My heart started beating loudly. It was time. He looked up and expected a friendly suburban parent kind of chat. "Hey. How you doing?"

"I know you."

"Yeah?" He looked quizzically at first. I was wondering if it was because I was twenty years older and pregnant or if it was an act to stave off any potential confrontation.

"Do I look familiar?"

"Yes." Now he furrowed his Angry Bird brows and looked at me more closely.

"I'm Joanna. You don't know who I am?"

I couldn't tell if the sudden recognition was fake and he pretended to just now figure out who I actually was or if he had known all along. "From New Rochelle, right? Your dad had an apartment on the top floor? Yeah, yeah, I remember you." He paused before asking, "How are you?"

I stared at him with as much intensity as I could muster.

And that was it. I couldn't do it anymore. Any of it. I couldn't be in the same room. I couldn't look in his face. I couldn't give him my words. And it was no longer because of fear. It was about worthiness. He didn't deserve my words, my feelings, my confronting him in an elementary school. In that moment, I became so present to something so revelatory. I knew what happened. I knew the act of the rape and the money and jewelry that was stolen. And then I knew the story that my mind and soul had written after it to survive and heal.

First it was the story of trauma and trying to figure out how to get past the bad dreams and the feelings of unease. Then I edited the manuscript to forgive, release and be grateful for what led to an incredible life. The event had remained the same, but I was the author of the impact. Tao had always said that while we don't have control over what happens to us, we always have control over our response. But never for a second did I consider the version he had written for himself in order to live with what he had done. Because how else do you go from raping a girl to being a father to one? How do you hold a girl down by her neck as you enter her and then go on to defend your country? How do you live with such unkind choices?

Suddenly I was hollow. I noticed that Jax was inventing a game with a group of boys and that Tash was off doing her thing and realized that we could leave without disappointing either. I didn't know what to do next, but I knew this was over. It was finally over.

"Tash, come on my love."

"No. I want to stay."

"Would you rather stay or go to the movies on a special Mommy Tashi date?"

"Movies. Movies. Can I get popcorn?"

"Of course."

"Candy?"

"Don't push it."

We kissed Jax and hurried out the door. Right before leaving, I glanced and noticed him staring at me. And I knew he knew. Whatever story he had written, seeing me had him questioning it.

When I got to the car, I called Mike. Since the call was over the car's Bluetooth, I was careful with my words.

"Are you okay, Babes?"

"No."

"Do you want to talk about it?"

"I don't think I can. Tashi and I are going to go to the movies now."

"Oh good."

"Dude. I thought I was fine. I mean, I AM fine. I know I am fine."

"Then why are you crying Mommy?" my daughter interjected.

Her words froze me. I was trying to make my voice sound normal, but was more like sobbing my way through the conversation. Natasha usually would have kept to her coloring books in the backseat, too engrossed in them to care about what I said on calls.

"Oh lovey. Mommy is just emotional. I'm so happy I got to take you to Jax's school thing today."

"It's okay, Mommy. I know why you're crying. Daddy said the baby in your belly makes you laugh and cry and pee a lot."

With that, we went to the movies. Though not realizing how spent the emotions of the afternoon had left me, I held Natasha on my lap and proceeded to sleep through most of it.

The following week, I was assisting Tao at an event about her life. We were doing these kinds of gatherings with increasing frequency: talks about her life as opposed to yoga-based workshops. I still loved watching the impact she had on the people who attended. Blown away by her presence and filled up by her wisdom, they left forever shifted. After we presented a slideshow of her real life Forrest Gump-like journey, there was a Q and A session. About thirty minutes into her answering questions, I suggested that we had time for one more. I noticed a sweet looking woman in the front who was timidly raising her hand. When I indicated that she could go ahead and ask her question, her face lit up. She asked her question but wasn't on a mic so I repeated it more loudly for Tao.

"Tao, this woman said that she has seen you on a lot of interviews and that you have inspired her so much. She hears you mention that there is nothing we cannot do. She wanted to know, beyond that, if there was any motto that you live by."

"Well. First, thank you for the question. I love questions and how they spark curiosity within us. I have a lot of silly ideas, really. But they have helped me throughout my life and it's why I am about to make 100 years old. I don't know why people make such a thing of it. To me, 100 is just another number."

With that, a murmur of laughter spread through the room. She continued.

"Procrastination is the only sin. We always think we have more time but the only time we know we have is now. Do not put off until tomorrow the things you want to do. Tomorrow never comes. One minute after midnight is already today again. So, whatever you want to do, do it NOW. This was something I always believed in, but I learned even more about it from my second husband, Bill. He was a good man. He did a lot of things to help people. But when it came time to doing the things he wanted to do for himself or for us, he always put that off. He finally agreed to go back to India with me again and then he died right before it. Don't do that. Don't think of an idea for so long that it's no longer possible. Do it."

CHAPTER ELEVEN

"There is nothing we cannot do. For we are not the doer, we are the instrument. And even the word impossible has the truth within it: I'm possible. Everything is possible."
—Tao Porchon-Lynch

Pregnant at 40 gets interesting. You hear doctors say things like "advanced maternal age" or my favorite, "geriatric pregnancy." In the days of political correctness, there are euphemisms for everything, except this. Just once, I wanted to hear that I was having a "wise pregnancy" or even "experienced" would do. But nope. As the months went on, I was told that I was high-risk and that while I could keep teaching yoga, I should limit my personal practice. Something was happening with my ovaries and they were concerned that twisting or other physical activity could lead to problems. Nevertheless, I continued to assist Tao as much as possible. She was seeming less physical as of late. Though still dancing and teaching and wearing her heels, there were some notable differences now. Where she used to lead six-hour workshops in one day and leave still raring to go, I began to notice that a one-hour class would leave her fatigued. And her cute little Smart car that she used to drive all over town was now gone so we created a schedule among a close circle of friends to drive her to appearances and rehearsals.

Back in Colorado on another family ski trip, Mike and I were walking through the beautifully quaint, snow globe-looking village of Vail holding hands. Being knocked up relieved me of the pressure of trying to finally make it as a snowboarder. The center of Vail looks like one part Switzerland and one part scenery in *Shrek*. Each building was architecturally gorgeous and adorably ski-ish. Natasha was off with her cousins and it was a rare moment on a huge family trip when Mike and I found ourselves alone.

"Dude, what should we name this baby?"

"I don't know, Jo. I haven't really thought of anything. But don't go too weird on me."

"Why? Natasha Tao is an awesome name. I didn't go too weird!"

"Yeah, but you wanted Om for a middle name at one point. Or Love."

"It's going to be hard to think of something as meaningful as Tao."

"True. I know you want ideas but I'm really not sure. We spent so much time trying to get pregnant that I haven't even thought about names for this one."

"What about Vail for the middle name?"

"Vail? I like Vail."

"I mean, we got engaged on top of Vail Mountain. It reminds us of love. It sounds strong and we like one syllable middle names. You dig it?"

"Sure. Vail's cool." Mike often made big life decisions with the same tone and enthusiasm as one ordering a sandwich.

"Do you like it for a boy or a girl?"

"Either I guess."

"Me too. Okay, cool. We just picked our baby's middle name. Now we only have one name left."

It was in this lighthearted mood on this refreshing walk that I got the call.

Tao had fallen and re-injured the troublesome hip. She would need surgery. At 99! This was a procedure they would typically question when someone was in their 80s and flat out refuse for anyone in their 90s. Luckily though they realized that Tao wasn't typical. Having a hip replacement at 99 would mean anesthesia, and anesthesia at that age would likely result in memory loss. Tao was given this information and made her choice. She said if she couldn't dance and couldn't teach yoga that she wouldn't be living anyway and that she wanted the surgery. She refused to be told by anyone else what she should do, even by her own body. As she had said on many occasions, her body was not the boss. She was. And she would tell it what to do.

I was feeling worried even though I didn't want to. I felt too far away geographically and too out of control spiritually. The whole family was skiing during the day, they would go to happy hour before dinner and pass out for the night shortly after it. I, on the other hand, was wide awake after the dishes were cleared. Natasha was always the cousin that kept the others awake on every sleepover or vacation. Even though she needed to rest up for the next day of ski school, I knew I could count on my girl to do an activity with me to take my mind off the worry and onto creativity.

I decided it was time to do a new vision board and to teach Tash the value of having a vision and then making a tangible representation to manifest it. This was her first attempt and I was unsurprised to see that much of hers focused around things she wanted to get more than who she wanted to be. Such is the nature of a vision board of a five-year-old. I explained to her that I had been making these for years and that they really work. She was excited as we collected images on my laptop and used the printer in the rental house to print them out and arrange on a paper.

"Mom, you need to put pictures of our new baby."

"You're right lovey. But we don't know if it's a boy or a girl, so I found pictures like this." I showed her a silhouetted image of a family of four. Then asked, "What's that one representing for you?"

"It's a front flip, Mom. I want to learn how to do a full flip this year. I also want to create a land of LOL dolls and I want to go to Hawaii and I want a puppy. I want to go to Disney World. And Hogwarts. And I want to ride a bike without training wheels."

The best part of parenthood is listening to the magic that comes out of your kids' mouths. The LOL dolls—silly little figures that are cleverly marketed so little kids enjoy opening them more than actually playing with them—had taken over our playroom. I was pretty sure that that could count as her creating a "land of LOL dolls" but I didn't say as much.

"I love it all Tashi. Just remember, you can put the front flip here but then you also have to practice. It takes both: vision and action."

"Who's that guy, Mommy?"

"That's Tony Robbins, Love."

"Uh oh. Is that who you want to marry next, Mom?"

I laughed before answering. "No Lovey. I don't want to marry Tony Robbins. I want to be married to Daddy! I don't love him like I love Daddy. Daddy's My Dude. I do love him though. He helps a lot of people and teaches them to live their best lives. Like Tao."

"Is that why you are putting him next to Tao on your board?"

"I am putting him next to Tao because I have a goal to introduce the two of them."

"Why?"

"Because they are both such world changers and they both are so lit up and special. I think they would really like each other. And hey, if you introduce two magical people, you double the magic, right?"

"So why don't you just call Tony Robbins and say 'My name is Joanna. Do you want to meet Tao?'"

"That would be a great idea, but I don't have his number, Baby. Tony Robbins is super famous. The cool thing though is you don't have to know how it's possible when you put something on your board. You put down WHAT you want. You don't have to control HOW it happens."

She thought about that for a bit as she taped a litter of kittens onto her board.

"I don't want to tell you what to put on yours, Tashi. But, Aunt Jen and Uncle Jonny are really allergic to cats so we won't be getting one anytime soon."

"Mo-om." Every kid knows how to say this in a way that stretches out the syllables. "I don't have to know HOW I'll get the kittens. I just have to put them down."

Touché, Tash. Touché.

When we got home from Colorado, I went straight to the rehab center to see my girl. Tao had been there before, and I knew the routine. I signed in with the nice woman at the reception desk and passed the chatty parrot in its cage. Tao didn't like being in any hospital or rehab center. She didn't like ever feeling restricted. When they took her down the hall to the physical therapy center, she would often feel offended if they asked her the questions they typically asked of older people. She would subtly show off by lifting the good leg over her head, hoping to quiet their doubts regarding her ability and range of motion. She inspired everyone with whom she came into contact. The staff often visited her when they weren't on duty. This helped because Tao did not like to eat with the other residents. Many were in severely limited states and she preferred to be in the company of the visitors who flowed in and out of her room bringing flowers, chocolates and conversation. But if she had to be in a facility, she did appreciate the vitality that the parrot and the other parakeet brought to the ward.

I said hi to the parrot and slowed as I neared the door. The last time she had been here, I was unprepared to see her in such a weakened state. Today, I paused to take a breath and allow my body and soul to fill with Tao's light. Whatever condition she was in, I would be ready to be her rock. I opened the door and was surprised to see that I had come in what must have been a lull between visitors. Tao was in bed, taking up an impossibly tiny amount of space. She usually wore her salt and pepper colored wig. Now, she looked like an angel. Her naturally all white, wispy hair was pulled back into a small bun and she looked beautifully at peace. The sun shined through the horizontal blinds and danced across her face. Her lips were slightly upturned at the corners as if she were smiling as she dreamed. *Amazing*, I thought. *She looks just as beautiful and magical even with her sparkly-blue eyes closed.* The thing about Tao is that she wanted to give those around her whatever they needed. She didn't take well to the role of patient and would instead spend her time mostly entertaining and always inspiring, the nurses, orderlies and doctors.

Knowing this, I decided not to wake her and disturb what had to be a much-needed rest, and took the items out of my bag. I had learned a trick over the years of how to get her the treatment she preferred. Typically a medical marvel, yet there were times where Tao would display human conditions and need medical intervention. When that happened and someone read her chart, they usually saw her age and made certain presumptions. To offset those, I would tape to the wall images of Tao in her signature yoga poses, fully demonstrating her strength and her magic. I also added some of the drawings done by Tao's namesake, my daughter. Natasha had made a point to draw all of Tao's favorite animals and to do them in her favorite colors. As I hung the last one, Tao stirred and as she turned her head, her eyes met mine.

I sat on the bed next to her and took her small and finely lined hand in mine. Her hands were always cold, except for at the centers. She had always taught us that the energy centers in the middle of the hands and the middle of the feet joined up with the one in the solar plexus. Those were sources of heat and power. As our hands joined, I felt her heat and her power. Suddenly, I was less concerned than I had been when I walked in. My heart filled with the strength in her hand what I hadn't realized had been emptied by seeing her initially frail appearance. She struggled a bit to sit up higher and I helped her. I was grateful that as we chatted, she sipped a little juice and took some bites of chocolate. I told her all about our trip to Colorado and heard all about the kindness of the people who came to see Tao. She rattled off the familiar names of those so close to her: Susan and Lori, Suzanne and Bonnie, Fred and Regina, Joyce and Renee. I felt comforted that the names were coming so easily to her mind and by her eyes that became more and more animated as she took in the art newly taped to the wall.

"How is that little girl of yours?"

"She's good, Tao. She wanted to come with me today, but I told her she had to go to school."

"Oh. How did she take that? If she's like me, I bet she doesn't like to be told 'no.'"

"That's for sure. She said she could miss school and come see you because you're a teacher so that should count."

Her laughter made her seem a few years younger and so much healthier. "She has an answer for everything, doesn't she?"

"Oh yeah."

"And look at her art. It doesn't look like the art of a child. She has such ancient wisdom in her already. Do you feel it? Look how she uses color so boldly and the way she captures the soul of the animals."

"As she was drawing that, she asked what it felt like to be 100. Then she said, it's okay if I didn't know because she was named after you and would find out for herself. She's way too much, Tao. And I love it."

"And how is that new baby doing inside the belly?"

Before I was even conscious of them, tears filled my eyes. "Oh Tao. I am just so grateful. It took a while, and all the faith I have, to believe we would get here. Now that I'm pregnant, I just want everything to be okay."

"Dear, it will be. I don't know anything about babies, but I do know about you. Everything you do has beauty because everything you do, you do it with love. When you notice a worry or a doubt pop into your mind, you just touch that baby and remind it who its mommy is. You are meant to help people in this world. And whoever this baby is, they chose you for a reason."

I took her tiny hand and asked if she would give the baby some magic. As I placed it on my ever-expanding bump, a feeling of calm washed over me. I suddenly knew that everything would be okay. Just as I took a breath and closed my eyes, it happened.

The baby did a decisive and powerful kick and Tao let out a delighted squeal. "Was that the baby? Oh, how wonderful! I've never felt a baby kick before. What energy to be that active already. It's as if the tiny baby is saying 'I have things to do in this world and I'm ready.'"

I left Tao in better spirits than I found her and for that, I was grateful. It wasn't lost on me that we were now playing with house money. At almost 100 years old, she was in what would be considered extra innings for most lifespans. I had always treated this sacred relationship with the appreciation it deserved, but now even more so. Every time I left Tao, I made sure to tell her how much I loved her, and I took a moment to take in and fully receive the magic of her gaze and the intensity of her warmth.

Her recovery went better than expected and three months later, Tao was back to most of her activities. If you didn't know her well, you would simply marvel at all the things she would say and all that she could do. If you were part of her inner circle though, you would have begun to see more changes. In one of her Sunday classes, when she taught the same posture a few times in a row, Renee and I caught one another's eyes and subtly helped shift Tao's focus to the next pose. We noticed that she repeated the same phrase a number of times within that class. From then on, we, along with a handful of other senior teachers who Tao had certified and trusted, would help her gently guide the classes.

We worked it out so that one or two of us would sit next to her to demonstrate the poses that were a bit demanding of her. And we positioned another one or two of us in front of her to subtly jog her memory. If she did a stretch on one side, the teacher in front of her would shift to the next as a reminder to change sides. If that didn't work, then one of the teachers next to Tao would suggest we do that pose on the other side. This was usually met with a dismissive response by Tao saying that she was just about to do that. Overall, our little secret army of Tao's helpers were committed to making it possible for her to continue teaching and to also protect the experience for those coming to see this guru.

For the most part, we were effective. Most of the people who attended class were too blown away by being in her presence to notice that there was any memory loss. Those who did, would often thank us after, either in person or email, for helping to so respectfully assist while not taking away any of the attention or light that was focused on Tao. Those were my favorite compliments, the ones reinforcing the belief that our efforts were working. It was all about Tao and sharing her light and her message with those coming to see her.

My personal practice was looking pretty comical at this point. Ironically, I was less restricted now that I was in the beached whale phase of pregnancy. My doctor was no longer concerned about the possibility of my ovaries twisting and I was given the green light to do what felt okay. He said that as a teacher, I knew my body and should trust what it could do. Certain poses like twists and lying flat on my back were still ruled out because they aren't as comfortable nor safe to do after week 20. At this point, I loved the added flexibility that I felt in my hips as they were opening in preparation for birth. I remembered this from the first time and really loved to practice the poses that opened them even more. Balance postures were funny to see because I looked so awkwardly front-loaded. But the best was when I did headstands. I had swelling in my ankles and feet and found relief when I would go upside down. It was like shaking the salad dressing bottle so that the good stuff was no longer just pooling at the bottom. As with my first pregnancy, my super pregnant headstands horrified some, inspired others and somewhere in the middle shocked most.

But this morning, I was too excited to feel my breath. It was getting away from me as if it was taking flight and giving new meaning to the notion of having "butterflies." I was doing a short, home yoga practice in my living room as Mike and Natasha were out at swim class. My breath was shorter, my thoughts scattered and even the baby was acting funny. Anytime I paused, the baby moved. Not just a bit of an elbow poking or a little foot kicking, this kid was wildly rolling over like it was performing an in utero interpretative dance.

After my shower, my hands were jittery as I did my makeup. Opting for a flowy dress, naturally smoky makeup and a blow out/flat iron combination for my hair, I was ready. I looked in the only mirror that was full length and felt satisfied. My face was fuller than usual, so I did a bit of natural contouring to bring my cheekbones back to life. My hips were wider, my boobs were bigger. I decided that the best I could shoot for was an "Earth Goddess" look and was pretty much hitting the mark.

To celebrate my 40th birthday that had come and gone, my mom had gotten me the greatest gift ever! I was about to spend the weekend at a huge Tony Robbins event. Having followed his work for so long, it was strange that this would be the first time I would experience it live and I couldn't wait. The anticipation was making it that much sweeter. The only thing that I had to promise my mom in return was that I would not walk on fire while pregnant.

I had been to the Prudential Center in New Jersey for a variety of events: the second date Nets game with Mike, Disney on Ice with Natasha and Mike, a Def Leppard concert. But this was a totally different feeling. The arena was set up so that the VIP ticket holders were all on the floor. Immediately surrounding the floor seats to one side was a reserved section for our large group. My friend who had arrived early saved me the seat that was in the first row of this section all the way on the aisle. This was key as she knew that at eight months pregnant, bathroom breaks would be a frequent occurrence. Gratefully, as I was making myself comfortable and situating my many snacks and water bottles, one of the members of the crew began chatting with me.

"Is this your first event?"

"It is. I'm so excited. Actually, WE are so excited." I held the bump and allowed the excitement to wash over me. It's always special to enjoy in real life what you imagined in your mind. In fact, one (Tao) might say that nothing incredible actually ever happens without it beginning as inspired thought.

"You are going to love it!"

"Have you been to a lot?"

"Yes. The first event I went to changed my life. Or, I should say, the event inspired me, and I changed my life. So now, I volunteer at them so that I can experience it myself and to also make it that much better for new people."

"That's awesome. I'm so happy you're in this section. I'm Joanna."

"I'm Matt. Nice to meet you, Joanna. And just so you know, the bathroom is all the way at the top of the stairs you just walked down, but," he added, "I'm going to show you the private bathroom for the VIPs that you can use. It's just down these two steps and back through that private door."

"Oh my God, Matt. That's so nice of you! Thank you. Thank you. Giving a pregnant chick easy access to a bathroom is like giving a non-pregnant chick diamonds and chocolate. Ohhhh, I shouldn't have said that. Now I want chocolate."

Matt laughed and his kind, green eyes crinkled as he did. I took him up on his offer to show me where the bathroom was and met a few kind attendants on the way. Everyone was smiling and happy and it made me that much more excited for the event to start.

Tony Robbins does not motivate people. In fact, he speaks to that notion as being a false premise. People are rarely outwardly motivated. Motivation is an intrinsic experience. Instead, he believes that you can help someone figure out the WHY behind their actions on a level that can inspire lasting and impactful change. I love that. I also love that he believes in active learning as opposed to passive learning. You cannot sit in a conference for hours and receive information as effectively at the end as you did in the beginning. With that in mind, he uses movement and music to create energy and establish the mood.

Fittingly, the weekend began with concert-like lighting and loud, happy dance music. Dancers came out on the stage and got the entire arena on their feet. I pushed myself out of my seat and began to move and sing. I felt my heartbeat quicken and a smile spread across my face. Already a mom this time around, there weren't as many times that I would find myself pausing to do something as organic and natural as dancing with my baby. With my first pregnancy, it was easier to take the time to do things like that. This felt amazing and lighthearted. There are moments when I meditate, and my mind stills, and I feel absolutely present. This was like that. I felt happy and grateful and excited, surrounded by like-minded friends and about to learn from someone whose work I admired. I had a healthy, happy boy or girl inside of me having their own dance party too. I was feeling the magic.

The different colored lights got more intense, the music got louder, the crowd got rowdier and just at the crescendo of it all, Tony Robbins ran onto the stage, beaming a radiant smile and pumping his fist. The buildup worked. If anyone was still in their seats, by this time they were now jumping out of them. We all felt so energized that by the time we sat back down, we were actively ready; mind, body and spirit, to receive the information and benefits from the weekend of personal development. Active learning.

As I sat, I reached for my water and settled in. The lights were brighter now. Less like a concert, people now held notebooks and pens on their laps. I was at the stage where my lap was a thing of months past, so I decided to sit empty-handed and simply be present. Within the first ten minutes of welcoming us to the event, Tony left the stage to walk the aisles, connecting more closely with the crowd. By doing this, he was able to make the huge arena feel intimate. My seat was directly in front of the aisle that separated the first group of VIP seats from the second. Tony walked to that aisle and turned to his left, mic-ed up and speaking as he strolled. It struck me that had he turned to his right and kept walking, he would walk directly into me. Like face-to-face smack into me.

I love watching people do their craft with mastery. Like seeing LeBron play basketball, Tao teach yoga, P!nk sing, I was enthralled watching Tony Robbins speak. Many people consider public speaking to be one of their biggest fears. I happened to love public speaking and the chance to learn from someone as masterful at it as Tony is was as exciting to me as the content itself. I knew he was tall but in person, he was even taller. Dressed in all black, he had the physical presence of a retired football player who was still in game shape. His smile accounted for much of his face, and went all the way to his eyes which shined with delight. This was a man who was living his path. Watching him in real life or seeing him super close-up on the jumbo screens positioned throughout the arena, it was clear that Tony was in the moment. He must have done thousands of events like this. I knew from seeing his schedule online that his itinerary was jam-packed and yet, seeing him in person opening this first session of the weekend, he had the gift of making you feel like this was the only moment there ever was.

He talked about what gave someone charisma: the ability to use eye contact, tone of voice and energy to connect with individuals in groups large or small. As he got on this topic, he turned and began walking in the direction where I was seated, and I felt it. With every fiber of my being, I knew that Tony Robbins was walking TO ME. I knew we were going to connect in a significant way. I knew that, in the midst of 15,000 people, we were about to have a meaningful interaction.

Before I could even finish thinking that thought, he was mid-sentence, still espousing on what makes those with charisma, charismatic, and suddenly immediately in front of me distracted by the watermelon I had smuggled in underneath my tight colorful sundress.

"Oh wow! Baby! Look at you."

The irony was not lost on me. Here was a man speaking about what makes someone have "it," and as soon as he locked eyes on me, I felt every bit of his fire, passion and love. He was joy-filled and childlike in his wonder and enthusiasm about life. He took my hand in his, and from nowhere, an assistant materialized handing me microphone. Our interaction was now being projected onto all the huge screens.

"How far along are you?"

"Eight months."

"Fantastic. Do we know what we're having? A boy or girl?"

"Nope. We're going for the surprise."

"Is it your first?"

"The second."

"Okay, so you're a pro. That baby is going to be rocking and rolling this weekend."

This conversation happened in a moment and all while we were still holding hands. As soon as our eyes met and our hands connected, I felt love. Not in a romantic sense, but in the way that I felt when I was with Tao. I knew that he was everything I had always hoped he would be: someone in love with his life's path. My goal of connecting the two of them was now even stronger than ever and I somehow, in my core, knew that this moment, materializing seemingly out of nowhere, was the first step in manifesting it. A friend sitting nearby had snapped some pics of the conversation both in real life and as shown on the jumbotron. I texted one of them to Mike.

Me: Dude. Tony and I totes just had a moment. Or maybe I should say Tony and our baby just totes had a moment.

Mike: Awesome. Cool pic. I'm sure you must've loved that.

Me: This event is awesome ... and it's only the first morning. I feel like this is the beginning of connecting him with Tao. I feel it. Out of 15,000 people here, he already FOUND ME!

Mike: Cool Babes. I'm sure you're going to have the best time. Just make sure you drink enough water. Okay, I'm playing UNO with Tash. She said LOVE YOU MOMMY. Peace.

His casual response was twofold. First, Mike is very accustomed to me being super excited about everything. Second, over the years that we had been together, he had definitely gotten used to the weird, cool things we had manifested individually and as a couple. Not sure if he would admit to such a thing, but I was pretty convinced that my expectation that things would always work out for us was rubbing off on him.

The rest of the day was filled with interesting topics about personal development, exercises that could be done with a partner, inspiration and many dance breaks. At times, Tony would have us all stand up and move, and before we could sit down again we were told to high five ten people or give them hugs. The event was so well organized, you could tell how much thought and attention was put into providing an experience of excellence for the attendees. The whole evening session was leading up to the fire walk, the one thing I had promised my mom that I wouldn't do. I kept my word and instead focused on cheering for my friends. As a source of inspiration before going outside where the hot coals were set up in a parking lot, Tony showed a video of a man in his 80s who was an inspiring example of health and vitality. Watching it, I thought it was another sign that I was moving in the direction of my goal. If he was inspired by this awesome man in his 80s, imagine how he would feel meeting Tao at almost 100!

We were about to pack our things and file out of the arena to the adjacent lot for the fire walk when Matt so kindly checked in with me. "How you feeling?"

"Awesome. I'm a little bummed not to do the fire walk though."

"That just means you'll have to come back. And don't worry, walking across the burning coals is really just a metaphor of what's possible. You can get all the magic of the weekend without it."

"Thanks Matt."

"That was cool with the chat you guys had on the big screen before."

"It was. I manifested it. I have this mentor and she's about to be 100 and she's the world's oldest living yoga teacher and competitive ballroom dancer. She marched with Gandhi and Dr. Martin Luther King, Jr. and she's magical. I've had it on my vision board to introduce her and Tony."

"Oh my God. She sounds amazing. And right up Tony's alley. He loves older people. He likes to interview them and highlight their pearls of wisdom at events like this."

"That's what I was thinking in that last video they showed."

"Joanna, you know what you should do?"

"What?" When someone is trying to help you along your way, LET THEM!

"Write a note to Tony tonight and I'll make sure I get it to his security guys who'll get it to him. He loves notes like that, and he'll definitely read it."

"Wow. Really, Matt? Thank you. I've had this vision so clearly for so long that I just KNEW it would happen. I've been trying not to get stuck on the how. Thank you so much for helping me with the how."

"Yeah, sure, no problem. I mean obviously I have no idea what will come of it but I'm happy to help. It sounds like your teacher is amazing and I think Tony would love to meet her. So, why not?"

With that, I, along with thousands of other people from all over the world, went outside to the Prudential Center parking lot in the middle of Newark, New Jersey to walk over burning coals. The energy was electric. Instead of focusing on what I couldn't do personally, I committed to finding joy and excitement in watching everyone else. It was really cool to witness. People would question if they could really do it right up until the moment they were about to go. Something would come over their face like a shield of calm. They were in state and ready to use their mind more powerfully than their bodies. Then once they'd finished walking across the burning coals, they'd experience pure joy. Watching the transformation from doubt to worry to confidence to focus to elation was so cool. Almost as cool as doing it myself. Almost.

That night I was fired up (pun intended)! I was so excited about writing to Tony telling him of Tao that I could think of little else. I wrote the note and was finally satisfied with my description. Summing up Tao's magic in note form was to condense a century of impact on one sheet of paper.

The next day was just as inspiring as the first and I gave the note to Matt to pass along. Out of my hands and out of my control, it was time to release with faith (see 4 Steps to Manifesting Anything in chapter ten). That is until I realized I had completely forgotten to put my contact information on the note! Holy pregnancy brain Batman! It really is a thing! I spent so much time thinking of phrasing everything perfectly and I forgot to add my contact info!

I tried to find Matt, but didn't see him. Then, during one of the breaks, a woman approached me: "It IS you!"

Immediately, I recognized her. She went to my gym and often did work on a laptop by the pool or in the café. Jerry Seinfeld once talked about this. There are people who are "extras" in the movie of your life, and you won't always notice them until you see them in a place out of context. This was a woman I had noticed. She had a presence that made you notice: powerful, strong, confident. I wasn't surprised to see her here with a young man who I was guessing was her son. People with powerful energy often took the time to develop themselves personally.

"Hi. You go to Life Time, right?" I asked her.

"Yes. I recognized you from the jumbotron yesterday and was figuring out which side of the arena you were on to come say hi."

"I'm Joanna. It's nice to officially meet you."

"I'm Joelle. I had to come over when I saw you were pregnant. This is my son, Jackson. He's 18 now but I remember being at this same event when I was pregnant with him and it was such a cool experience."

"Oh, I'm so glad you found me. How nice to meet you." Then turning to Jackson, "And how cool that you come as an adult to do this with your mom! So, in about 18 years, this little one'll be here with me too, right?" Her tall son smiled politely in response.

Joelle continued, "I used to work with Tony for years. We're good friends and I love coming to events when I can. It doesn't always work schedule-wise but when it does, I come."

"That's awesome. How long did you work together?"

"For years. He actually walked me down the aisle when I got married."

"How cool."

Again, when someone is put on your path like a billboard pointing to your destination, TAKE NOTICE! I filled her in about Tao and her face alit with inspiration.

"Wow, she sounds so special. Tony would definitely love her. He's really committed to listening to and preserving the stories of inspiring older people."

I told her about the note and about my blunder.

"Do me a favor. Send me an email and write whatever you wrote in the note and I'll make sure Tony gets it."

"Oh my God, thank you. This means a lot. I've meditated on the two of them meeting for so long. I really appreciate you finding me today."

"Hey, out of the thousands of people here, it can't be an accident that you were on the big screen and that I'd recognize you from the gym even though we'd never met there. So, whatever this turns into, it's obviously meant to be. Happy to help."

"Thanks, Joelle. And so nice to meet you, Jackson."

With that, they excused themselves to find a bathroom before the next session began.

CHAPTER TWELVE

*"Do not give in to fear. As soon as a fearful thought enters your mind,
choose love, beauty, nature. Where those are, fear cannot exist."*
—Tao Porchon-Lynch

Could peeing count as a full-time job? That was my deep thought of the morning as I sat on the toilet. Sometimes I sat for a bit longer than necessary out of the combination of comfort and fatigue. Well, "comfort" was definitely a relative term. Nine months pregnant and it was my third time peeing and I had only been awake for an hour. The waddle to the bathroom made me dream of an en suite situation each time, so for this trek I actually brought my phone for company and entertainment. I was about to do a YouTube search for a morning meditation that I could listen to as I started the day to give a bit of positive "inspo" whilst brushing my teeth. When I entered the passcode to unlock my phone, an email alert scrolled across the top. All I saw was Hey Joanna! It's Tony Robbins!

Since attending his event the month before, I was on an email list so seeing messages from Tony Robbins or one of his related companies wasn't unusual. I assumed this was an announcement for a course he was offering online or a promotion for an event somewhere fabulous like Fiji (both things that I had been considering). I opened the email.

It was neither.

Thanks for your special note Joanna! I would love to meet Tao!
Would she like to come to the Unleash the Power Within event in Palm Beach Florida November 9 through the 11th? We could meet and have lunch in the middle of the program on the 10th.

If this works my assistant who is copied above can coordinate comple-
*mentary VIP tickets and arrange a meeting on the 10*th *as well. Just reach*
out directly to her if the schedule works. I look forward to meeting you both!
Namaste!

Tony

In times of excitement or fear, I typically react by jumping up and down and cursing. The first was no longer an option because it only served to exaggerate the second.

"Holy fucking shit! Holy fucking shit! Duuuuuude! Oh my God!"

Nothing.

"Duuuuuude!"

No response. I finished brushing my teeth, spitting out the toothpaste too vigorously and splashing the mirror. It would typically bother my world to not clean that up before leaving the bathroom, but in this case I couldn't care less. I hurried as fast as my huge watermelon-belly would allow back to the bedroom. Mike was lying there as if the universe hadn't just completely aligned.

He looked up casually and asked, "What's up?"

"Dude! When your woman is 25 months pregnant screaming 'Holy fucking shit' from the bathroom, you're supposed to respond."

"I figured if you were having the baby, you would say that. And if you weren't, you'd tell me whatever it is when you got out. No big deal."

"Um. Tony Robbins just sent me an email! Like Tony himself. From his personal email."

My Dude actually sat up. "Awesome. What did it say?"

"That he'd love to meet Tao. He thanked me for the note and, oh my God!—what am I doing? I'll just read it to you."

Reading it out loud now for the second time made it feel even more real. "Do you know what this means? I mean besides the fact that we're basically best friends now. I wonder if I should call him Tone. I feel like we're there. But do you realize Duuuuuude! that Tao and Tony Robbins are going to meet. These world changers! My dream! It's happening!"

"It is! That's so cool, Babes. I know how long you've wanted this. I'm so happy for you. Though Babes, you do realize, right?"

"What?"

"He said November 9th to 11th."

"I know! My numbers. 11/11. How cool!"

"I meant that it'll be like three or four weeks after you have the baby, Babes. And the doctor already said you're probably having another C-section. Do you really think you can fly to Palm Beach so soon after you deliver? I mean, you'll be nursing. Would you take the baby?"

"I have to figure this out. Because it's happening. It's all happening. This is amazing. Holy shit! How nice was this of him? His schedule is crazy, and he took the time to personally write that and to invite us as his guest to his event."

"Do you think that event would be too much for Tao? You came home after that weekend excited and exhausted. And she's 99."

"I have to figure this all out. I do think the event would be a lot for her. She isn't into sitting for a long time and the loud music wouldn't be her thing either. But he mentioned coming in between sessions. I wonder if we could just fly to Palm Beach for the day. Especially if we leave right from Westchester airport. That would be doable."

"And the baby?"

"We'd have to bring the baby."

"We?"

"Yeah. This is all falling into place. You're totally going to have to come My Love. We can fly down to Palm Beach for the day. My mom can watch Tashi. So, you, Tao, new baby and me. To meet Tony Robbins. You know? No big deal. Just one of my magical mentors meeting another one." With that, I couldn't help it. I jumped up and down.

"Oh God, Jo. Please be careful."

"Yeah. That was a mistake. And now I have to pee again. But worth it," I called out as I waddled back to the bathroom.

Tao's words rang through my mind. It was so true. Everything is possible. The limits come from within. Whether we tell ourselves that something can or cannot come to be, we create it as our truth. I always saw this happening and now that it was in the works, I was even more committed to and more excited about the unfolding.

The next day, I brought Tao a grapefruit juice and a bagel. She was sitting in the living room of her apartment. It was in a tall building, and had a wall of windows through which she loved to look. From this view, she would watch the sunrise and say out loud that it would be the best day of her life. The interior of the apartment was filled with artifacts as interesting as she: photos of her husbands, a huge picture of Gandhi, souvenirs from different adventures, gifts from all over the world, and photos of Tao in every stage of life and with so many different friends. A framed photo of Renee wearing Tao's dress as she married Mike and me graced the entrance table, and a collage I made of my moments with Tao was on her windowsill. The picture of Tao holding Natasha Tao for the first time was right next to the couch. Being a string in the fabric that comprised the story of Tao's life and having that presence in her actual living space, was an unbelievable honor and one that I didn't take lightly. I felt so privileged to be among those welcomed into her home, her nest, her intimate moments. I placed my heavy bag on the chair and walked the few feet to the living area.

She looked absolutely radiant dressed in a flowy magenta skirt with jewels on it that was paired it with a long-sleeved magenta top. The requisite strappy black heels and big sparkly earrings completed her outfit. The light that shined through the window exaggerated the twinkle in her blue eyes and her smile lit up her face even more. She was gorgeous. And thin. Tao had always been very petite, but today she was noticeably thinner than usual. I couldn't help but note that the bone structure of her upper arms looked like they were the same size as my wrists. It was incredible that someone so strong could look so frail.

I sat across from her, and smiled when she actually took a bite of the bagel.

"Can I offer you anything?"

"No thank you, Tao. I was just drinking water in the car and these days, if I drink too much, I spend too much of my day in the bathroom."

Tao laughed easily. She always laughed easily and despite our nearly sixty-year age difference, when we were together, we giggled like silly little girls. Her company was easy. She was a great listener and the most interesting storyteller. Sometimes these days, Tao would repeat the same story in a visit. It was happening more often, so I chose to listen again as if hearing it for the first time and to focus on the gratitude I felt for her still being around to tell it.

"Tao, how are you feeling?"

"I feel good. A bit tired today. But better now that you're here."

"Did you dance today?"

"Yes. I did. We rehearsed for quite a bit. I have another competition coming up at the end of the month."

"I'm sure you will wow them as usual, Tao."

"I'm going to do a few different dances. One of them I do with two partners."

"Two partners. I'm not surprised that it now takes two young men to keep up with you."

"And if you add them together, I'm still double their age!"

"Tao, I wanted to talk to you about an opportunity we have to do something special together."

"Oh, good. I have too many people telling me things I can't do lately. I love that you always treat me like I can do anything."

"I've learned from the best. There's no way I would be so bold as to tell you what you can do."

The more distracted she was with the conversation, the more bites of the bagel and sips of the juice she took.

"So, Tao. There's a man called Tony Robbins and he does a lot of great work in the world."

"Oh, is he a friend of yours?"

"Not yet, but I'm working on it."

"Well, if you like his energy, the universe will bring him into your life."

"It already has. I've been following his work for years and I'm a fan of what he does. He helps people take action and create the life they imagine. He reminds me of you—not in method but in result. And he's committed to helping feed the hungry. He's already helped feed over a billion people. Here, I'll show you a picture of him."

I opened Google and did an image search on his name. I found one that showed Tony's signature smile and turned the phone to Tao.

"He looks happy. And he has a sparkle in his eye. What a nice face. Are we going to do a workshop for him?"

"Well, he leads these huge personal development events. I went to one in New Jersey and there were 15,000 people there. He invited us to one in Florida."

"I love Florida. I spent a lot of time there when I was younger. And I love being by the beach. The ocean is always renewing itself. It's like watching the lungs of the Earth—bringing breath in with each wave and exhaling as it slips back. The rhythm of receiving and releasing is the perfect reminder of how we begin again with every breath. Are you sure I can't get you anything?"

"No thank you. I'm just happy to see you having something. So, I've had on my vision board for a while a picture of you and a picture of this man, Tony Robbins. Then when I attended his event, I met people who passed along a note to him from me. In the note, I told him all about you, and now he wants to meet you."

"How nice. Will he come to one of my classes?"

"He's not in New York. So, the first thing I wanted to do was to see if this is all okay with you. If it is, I will book us tickets to fly to Palm Beach for the day. It will be after I have the baby so we would go with Mike and the baby too."

"That sounds like fun."

"I'm really excited, Tao. He's super famous and I wasn't sure how I was going to manifest this, but in my heart I KNOW that the two of you were meant to meet."

"Then I'm not surprised you found a way. Life is like that. When you put something in your mind and meditate on it with clarity, it happens. And you do things with such joy, Dear. Joy speeds up the process of going from thought to thing."

"I like that … from thought to thing. Tao, I love you."

I took her hand in mine: delicate, small and lined with blue veins. Her nails shiny pink and expertly polished.

"I love you too," she answered. "I feel good when we're together."

"So do I, Tao. Are you sure this is okay though? You don't think it's too much to go to Florida for the day?"

"I don't know who your friend is but if you like him this much, that's enough for me. I always smile when we're together. And people have started to treat me like I can't do things. I'm not on this planet to sit around, you know. So I say yes."

"Then it's settled. We'll have an adventure."

I was online trying to book our tickets when I reached a hurdle. So accustomed to being able to do everything via the internet, I realized that this was an issue that required me calling an actual human. When the representative from the airline answered, I explained my issue.

"So you're trying to book a ticket for your baby?"

"Yes."

"Okay, well we consider children under the age of two to be lap babies and they do not require their own ticket."

"Yes, that much I know. Thank you. The issue is that when I went to book online, they needed the name and gender of my baby."

"Yes."

"But my baby hasn't been born yet and we aren't finding out the gender until then."

"Oh, how exciting. Congratulations! And no worries, Ma'am. We can go ahead and book the three adult tickets and when you have the baby, you can call back with the name and gender."

Wow. That phone call made everything even more real. Our tickets were booked! Mike, Tao, New Baby and me were flying to Palm Beach to go meet with Tony Robbins. And this kid was coming so soon. I started dreaming of that magical moment when I would meet my new baby, of the first time I would see with my eyes the person I had felt in my body and loved with my heart. I was ready for it all over again, ready for my heart, my home and our family to expand.

Tao taught me that miracles were happening everywhere and often, and that I mustn't forget to look for them. A new baby had come into my womb and would then come into this world riding one miracle on to the next.

My doctor had gone away on a golf trip and as a result my weekly appointment was switched from Friday to Monday. I shudder to think of the possible outcome had that not been the case. In hindsight, I don't think I've ever been so grateful for what I thought was the world's most boring sport. We had a scheduled C-section set for Tuesday, October 3rd. When you are given the choice as to when your miracle arrives, why not choose a date with your favorite numbers? Monday the 2nd was meant to be a low-key day to prepare. I was going for my last scheduled checkup, getting my hair blown out (for the hold-the-brand-new-baby close-up) and picking up Tashi from the school one final time before her world changed.

I could tell from the face of the nurse as she watched the monitor that something wasn't right.

"What's going on?"

"I'm not loving the activity. I'm going to see if rolling you over helps the baby move around." She adjusted the position of the ultrasound wand as she and Mike helped me roll onto my side. I caught his gaze. In moments like these, he may feel fear, but his face stays calm. The nurse still didn't seem happy with what the monitor was showing and left to get the doctor.

Mike came to my side and I took his hand just when the doctor strode in.

"So, what's going on, Joanna? We have a date for tomorrow. Why are you messing with the plan?"

"I know, Doc. This is supposed to be a quick visit. What's happening?"

He studied the monitor, his face revealing nothing.

"Is everything okay?"

"I don't love the activity right now. I'm going to send you over to the hospital."

Mike wanted answers. "Are we having the baby today, Doc?"

"Well, if the baby perks up, we can wait until tomorrow. If not, we'll do this today."

"I have a hair appointment at two o'clock. Should I cancel?"

"Let me see. Take off your hat."

I did.

"Don't cancel yet," he said with a smile. Let's see what happens at the hospital. I mean, your hair looks fine, Joanna. But don't cancel yet." He winked.

His lighthearted jokes helped. He was always dry and funny with us and I figured if he was joking, nothing was that serious. At least not yet.

The hospital was expecting us the next day. Mike's sister works there, and we benefited from that perk. For both deliveries, she had arranged for a private room and paired me with a nurse whose energy would be a match for mine.

Surprised to see us a day early, the staff jokingly said that they had no time to roll out our red carpet but would find us a private suite and our favorite labor and delivery nurse. Then my sister-in-law walked in, followed by Catherine, an Indian angel with her black hair in a ponytail and her sweet face wearing a warm smile.

"Joanna! Mike! I'm so happy to see you. When Kristine told me you were coming tomorrow, I was so sad to miss it. I'm always off on Tuesdays. Now we can have another baby together."

We hugged as close as my enormous belly would allow.

"So, do you think it's definitely going to be today then?"

"Let's see. We'll get you hooked up to the machine and see what this baby is up to. Okay, darling?"

After ten minutes of monitoring my activity and contractions, she confirmed that she thought the baby would have to come out today. Like with Natasha, the baby's heart rate was dropping with contractions. I sent Mike home for the "go-bag" and for him to eat and shower. I could deal with a C-section but doing it with a hangry Dude would be more than I could handle. But the moment he left, it seemed that the urgency amplified and I began to worry if he would make it back in time. My family was alerted. My sister-in-law Kristine was already changing into scrubs just in case.

Mike made it back just in time. I was given five minutes to fix my makeup. This bit of vanity may seem absolutely crazy, but I knew from the first time that the moment-of-birth picture would be something that I would have and treasure for the rest of my life. The post-baby glow that people would end up commenting about on Facebook had as much to do with well-placed bronzer as it did with pure joy.

We were wheeling into the O.R. and Catherine was holding my hand in hers as they took Mike to change into scrubs. He met me in there, and without warning, seeing him in that moment, tears began to stream down my cheeks.

"Why are crying Babes?"

"It's all happening again, Dude. Tell me everything is okay."

"Of course it is! We've been here before. You've done this before. We're about to meet our baby. Everything'll be fine."

His voice soothed me as much as it could've because I'd seen Catherine's face go from playful to more serious on the way to the O.R.

A C-section is a strange event. I was wide awake and yet my insides were outside as I lay on the table with my midsection open. Mike is too tall to not see over the curtain and too curious to ever look away. Watching his face watch a surgery is like watching someone else watch a scary movie. He kept saying things like, "Damn. You really can't feel this Babes? That's crazy!"

But you do feel it. While it may not be the pain you would feel without anesthesia, you feel intense pulling and tugging and a weird vacuum-like whoosh as they lift the baby out. The whoosh was still a few minutes from happening when it occurred to me that the doctor they had introduced and who was standing behind me was the neonatal intensive care unit doctor, or called the N.I.C.U. doc. I was straining to remember if they had one in the operating room when Natasha was born. *Is this normal or is something happening here?* I wondered.

Someone had suggested that we request a "gentle C-section" this time around. The name could be a misnomer as the only difference is that there are two curtains: the traditional blue one and a clear one behind that. So, right as the baby is being pulled out and revealed, the blue curtain would drop. This would more closely mimic a traditional birth in that Mike would be the first to see the baby and tell me the gender. To this day, his classy way of describing it is to say that all he saw were balls. The shock in his voice was audible as he yelled "BOY! And he's dark!"

The second comment didn't register as strange. Mike is half-Indian and people stopped us constantly to say what beautiful coloring Tash had. I chalked it up as the same. But unlike Natasha, our new baby wasn't immediately put on my chest. There was no playful energy asking what the name was or if Mike wanted to cut the cord. There seemed to be a sense of urgency as our new little boy was whisked into the hands of the N.I.C.U. doctor and then into his little incubator table behind us. I strained my neck to see what was happening behind me but to no avail, while Mike had positioned himself so that I could see him, and he could see our new child.

"What's going on? Dude, what's going on?"

The N.I.C.U doctor began to address us both. "Your little boy here is having a bit of trouble breathing." Then to just Mike, "You see his belly pulling in with each breath. He's working harder than we would want him to to breathe. We call that tugging."

It was hard to be on the table as they put me back together, especially since my gore was fully visible to Mike and his face showed it.

"Wow, Babes. It's crazy that you don't feel this. You have more stuff outside of you than in right now."

In fact I could no longer feel anything. Except the pressure was there. The tugging was there as they removed things like the placenta and replaced things like organs, and then the sewing to put me back together. All of that was happening but I no longer cared. I wanted my baby. My baby boy. I needed him. I felt like they had just severed my limbs and I wanted them back!

Then I heard a nurse say, "He's pinking up" and realized that the baby, our baby, was not dark from being part Indian. He was dark from not having been able to breathe! As they kept fussing about my lower half, one of the doctors held up the cord to explain that not only was it wrapped around our son's neck but there was also a "true knot" in it. Like a shoelace, they showed us the tightly knit knot of the umbilical cord and in that moment, I sobbed. How had our miracle lived and breathed with a knot in the cord and it wrapped around his neck? HIS! A boy. I still couldn't believe we had a son. A son I had yet to hold in my arms. My entire body, mind and soul was yearning with an unimaginable intensity to hold my baby.

I arched my neck and strained to see behind me. My mind raced: *they probably position the N.I.C.U stations so that mamas can't see in case of dire situations. Is this that? What is happening? Oh, God, please!*

"Mike. What's going on? How's our baby?"

"He's cute, Babes."

"What does he look like? I want him. Tell me things."

"He looks smushy and he's holding my finger and he's got a good grip."

The doctor interrupted. "You see that, Daddy? He's starting to get a bit pinker in color. That's what we're looking to see."

I couldn't see the doctor clearly, but I knew he could hear me.

"Is he going to have to go to the N.I.C.U?"

"Yes, he will. He's going to need a bit of our help. He's a strong and beautiful baby," he added as I began to sob.

"Does this handsome little guy have a name yet, Daddy?"

Mike and I hadn't yet fully agreed on a name for a boy. If it was a girl, we would name her Xenia Vail, and if a boy I was rooting for River Vail. Mike didn't love it, but he liked it. He had no better suggestion though. Just a week earlier I told him that I thought I would win by default. If I loved it and he liked it and he couldn't think of one he loved, I would probably win the name game. All of that had been forgotten until this moment.

Mike looked at me and I couldn't form words. I was too busy crying and praying. He never let go of our baby's hand as he asked me, "River"?

I nodded. He turned to the doctor and told him that our son's name was River.

The doctor answered, "We're going to take little River with us and help him."

This was it. No nursing. No skin to skin. They were taking our baby! Our River.

"WAIT! I need him. I NEED him."

Catherine, our angel, intervened. She quietly yet firmly grabbed the elbow of the N.I.C.U nurse who was now holding River. "The mom is a yoga teacher. You need to put River on her chest and let her breathe with him before you take him." The nurse mumbled something quietly and urgently. I heard Catherine respond, "You can take the baby in a minute. He needs his mama and his mama needs him."

It wasn't until that moment when I realized that the playlist I had made for the birth was still on in the background. A beautiful yoga song, *Longtime Sun*, was playing softly as they put my blanket-wrapped miracle on my chest.

I had no idea if my insides were back together. I had no idea about anything. All I knew for sure was that River was here. He was home. On my chest.

May the longtime sun shine upon you
All love surround you

The years of praying and the months of waiting all made this moment that much more sacred. His eyes opened and they met mine. His upper lip was jutting out more than his lower lip, just as it had been in every sonogram picture. This was my beautiful baby and he was finally in my arms.

And the pure light within you

Guide your way on

I looked at my son and spoke to him in mommy whispers for the first time:

"You are strong. You are powerful. You breathe with ease. You have everything you need. You are everything you need. Daddy and I love you so so much. So so much! Our sweet boy."

"Joanna, it's time. We have to take River with us," The N.I.C.U. nurse insisted.

"One more second ... please." I took in every inch of his face and felt his soft cheek on my lips. Then I kissed those lips for the first time. "Go breathe my love. And then come right back to Mommy. You are our special love." I held my hand to his chest and chanted "Ommmmmmmmmmmmmmmmmm.»

Guide your way on.

CHAPTER THIRTEEN

"I do not believe in age. I believe in energy. I feel that I haven't grown up yet."
—*Tao Porchon-Lynch*

We were each pushing precious cargo: Mike with the stroller and I with the wheelchair. Going through security at our small local airport was clunky, yet relatively easy. Mike had to hold River once the stroller was folded up and loaded on to the belt. I was pushing Tao in the wheelchair when the young security officer asked if she was able to walk through.

"What did you say, young man? Do I need to take off my heels?"

He glanced down and appeared to take in the woman who was dressed in a tight black top, a knee-length flowy black and white-striped skirt, black high heels and wrapped in a magenta shawl.

"No, Ma'am. You're perfectly okay right where you are."

Tao pushed herself out of the chair and skipped in her heels through the metal detector. The young man watched, mouth agape. Apparently, he had never seen a 99-year-old skip her way through his security line. But the machine beeped as she did and when he took the wand to her, Tao informed him that the Ganesh necklace she wore around her neck for over seven decades often triggered the alarm.

He waved his wand over it to confirm and as he did so, got a little lesson from Tao. "This is Ganesh. He has been with me longer than you have been alive. He's the remover of obstacles, especially with new ventures. You, young man, have a beautiful smile. And you take your time with each person, which is nice to see. Too many people are in a hurry, especially young people. Taking the time to smile and to greet people is the same as saying 'I love you' to each person you see. Thank you for being so kind with me today."

We reassembled the stroller, bought Tao a juice and sat in the boarding area. As I nursed River, I noticed that the man from security kept glancing at Tao while he spoke to his colleagues. He smiled as he talked, and I assumed by the looks of admiration that he was telling them all about her. She had gone on to tell him that not only was she 99 years old, but she was still teaching yoga and competing in ballroom dancing. This was Tao in all her glory, leaving in her wake awe and inspired people. We boarded the plane just as I finished nursing and strapped River into the baby carrier on my chest. As we took off, we left Westchester below and floated above the clouds.

Tao looked so peaceful in profile. "I love being above the clouds. They are so fluffy and filled with beauty. It looks almost as if you could put your hand out and touch them."

"Tao, you're so beautiful. You've seen so much in your life so far and you still look at everything like it's brand new."

"That is the secret, Dear. When you look at the world with wonder, you see a wonderful world. I never tire of looking at nature. It is my teacher. I have made it to almost 100, but the trees and the mountains and the oceans were here before I was, and they will be here after. I don't take one single minute for granted."

"Do you ever get tired?"

"A bit more than I used to. But I'm not ready to dance to the next planet yet."

"I have no worries about that, Tao. You're the most magical person I've ever known. I'm sure when you choose to 'dance to the next planet' it'll be because you feel complete on this one. I mean, how many people could even say they've lived as long or as rich a life as you?"

"I've been very lucky, I have had incredible people in my life who have always filled me with love and joy."

"I can't even imagine what it's all been like for you. You were here before cars, before phones, before all this technology. You've seen wars and have loved and lost two husbands. Has it been crazy to watch the world around you transform so much?"

"These days I see so many people, especially young people, looking like dinosaurs. They walk with their necks curved forward and their heads down staring into their phones. They're missing so much of the beauty. If your head is down, how do you see the clouds, the mountains, the face of your true love passing you on the street?"

"That part worries me too," I empathized. "Especially now as a mom. Mike loves technology and thinks it's all cool and exciting. I'm concerned that we'll lose our ability to connect as humans."

"That's why it's so important to have good teachers. We need good teachers to show the next generation what it means to be a community. That's where the energy of youth is so important. Our children are precious and if we teach them the importance of kindness, they can heal the world."

Tao returned her focus to the window and although she would never admit it, I saw her close her eyes and drift off. As soon as she did, I looked down at River sleeping on my chest and exhaled.

The first three weeks of his life had been a blur of appointments. He spent the first few days in the N.I.C.U. The day he was born, he was fed by an IV and his tiny body was hooked up to so many machines. They put a splint on one arm for the tubes to stay in place. He had a few hospital bracelets around an ankle and one with a barcode that matched the corresponding one on my bracelet. Every hour, the nurse and Mike wheeled me from my bed to the N.I.C.U. to hold River. Passing the other babies whose situations seemed far more serious, I silently prayed for them.

Logically, I wanted to feel grateful that we had a problem which could be solved and that I KNEW with every fiber of my being that my baby would be okay. Emotionally, I was holding my River though it was harder to connect with him this way than in the natural, skin to skin way that I craved. I was so aware of the tubes in his nose and the IV in his arm. I wanted to love and squeeze him but didn't want to hurt him. He looked so delicate in my arms. So small. Even that thought brought up so much guilt as some of the babies around us were less than four pounds. River was full-term and looked like the giant of the N.I.C.U. I tried, for the first time, hours after his birth, to nurse him. I knew from the last time that with C-sections, it could take a few days for my milk to come in. I wanted to nurse to help stimulate that. I wanted to nurse to help teach River how to latch. I wanted to nurse so that I felt assured that he was okay.

With every visit, another bit of his hardware was removed, and I was less and less restricted in my holding him, until finally, he was able to be with me in my hospital room. The relief I felt in having him with me was all-consuming and I never wanted to be without him again.

The second day, Natasha was able to come and meet her baby brother. She had spent the night at her Aunt Jen's and was loving the attention she was getting in kindergarten for her new baby. She introduced him to the rest of the family, and was so proud, even if he wasn't the sister she'd "ordered." We were a family of four. The family of four that had been on my vision board for years.

River was having difficulty nursing, an issue exacerbated by the fact that he was tongue-tied. We had that fixed with a laser procedure, but by that point, he was already losing weight and it was scary. I had an aggressive schedule that meant I was either nursing or pumping for about 20 hours a day. Sleep was only a memory. When doctors asked if I was getting any rest, I would simply laugh. Feeding River and praying for weight gain was my obsessive focus. Making sure that Natasha was getting the love she needed in this whole transition was next. Taking care of myself had fallen way to the bottom of the priority list. Mike questioned if we could even make the Florida trip still happen.

I looked across the aisle to see him sleeping with his laptop on the tray before him. I was so grateful that he was able to take the day off and help me make this dream a reality, but seeing the circles under his eyes, I also knew the sleepless nights were taking their toll. I was happy to see him sleep.

Before landing, the flight attendant asked if she could take a photo with Tao. She recognized her from a recent appearance on *Live with Kelly and Ryan* and had been following her ever since. Tao graciously obliged and offered up her sparkly-eyed smile.

Palm Beach was sunny and warm, and Tao exhaled the way she does whenever she is close to the ocean. Mike busied himself with putting the car seat into the rental car and then we were on our way. The people in charge of Tony Robbins' schedule told us that he was likely to have a window of time midday. They suggested that we wait at the gorgeous resort nearby. I was going on faith on fumes since I had no real solid plan from the people with whom I had been in touch via text. I had a baby that needed constant feeding and sleeping, and a husband who looked like he could still use both as well.

We busied ourselves having lunch in a restaurant positioned between the pool and the ocean. Tao ate more in that meal than usual, so we kept ordering more food. If nothing else happened on the trip, I already felt that seeing her enjoy food this much was a win! She and Mike smiled as they clinked their glasses of wine. When we offered her ice cream after her lunch, she happily agreed.

"Dear, your baby is so sweet. Is he like this all the time?"

"Yes, he really just eats, sleeps and cuddles all day. He's so so sweet, Tao. Now, we just have to help him gain weight."

"He will, Dear. I know nothing about babies, but I know you. You will do everything he needs, and he will change the world just like your little girl. How is little Tao with him?"

"She is the sweetest when it comes to him. Even though she says she asked for a sister." I loved seeing Tao laugh. Watching her in this moment, eating ice cream, having a glass of wine and laughing at the sassiness of her namesake, I felt whole.

After getting her a spa pedicure and a foot massage, I received a text that said Tony was ready and given the address to his house. We arrived and announced who we were to the call box before the gates opened. We drove up the driveway to a point where Tao and I got out of the car leaving Mike with a sleeping River, and were greeted by the assistant who had so kindly been texting me for weeks.

"I'm so happy to finally meet you in person, Joanna. And this must be the famous Tao!"

"Hello Dear, thank you so much for having us."

I loved that Tao still really didn't know where we were or why, but she trusted me and was leaning in to the adventure.

"I'm going to take you both around the side of the house into the backyard. Tony and Sage will be out to meet you in a few minutes. Can I get you water or anything?"

We politely declined the offer of drinks and I took Tao's arm in mine as we followed the assistant to the backyard. Along the way, we passed the small plunge pool that I had seen in a documentary that was part of Tony's daily routine. Seeing that plunge pool in real life made my breath catch in the back of my throat for just a moment. I was present to the miracle that was unfolding. The miracle didn't have as much to do with Tao or Tony Robbins per se. It had to do with the confirmation that whatever you can envision, you can create; whatever you can dream, you can do. This was one of those moments for me. This had gone from vision board fodder to actually happening in a matter of months.

We were seated on a sleek white couch on an vibrantly green lawn overlooking the ocean. The waves crashed loudly, and I wondered if it would be too noisy for Tao to be able to hear. I wanted her to feel comfortable and silently prayed that the wig she wore daily would stay put against any gusts of wind. I always marveled at the fact that it never moved even when demonstrating inversions or being flipped upside down during ballroom dances. That thought reassured me. I smiled at Tao and did a quick check of my enormous new mama boobs to make sure that they weren't leaking.

Vanity takes a backseat in the first weeks of having a new baby. Adding in my worries about River's feeding, I was lucky to shower most days. Being here, with people I had fantasized about meeting, the best I could muster was a flowy magenta skirt with a tight light-blue nursing tank covered in a loose black cross-front long-sleeved top. My hair was blown straight, another miracle. As for my face, there was little that makeup could do to cover the puffiness from the birth and the circles from so little sleep since. My saving grace was the joy I felt. I hoped that the happiness would add a glow that would shine energetically even though I wasn't feeling it physically.

After about ten minutes of enjoying the waterfront view, I glanced back to see Tony and Sage approaching from their home; he dressed all in black and she angelic in all white. We stood as they reached us and made introductions all around.

The two couches were set up in an "L" shape. Tao was seated in the innermost part of one of the couches and I sat next to her. On the other, Tony was seated as close to Tao as possible and Sage began on the couch next to him. As soon as Tao spoke, Sage quickly moved to a spot on the grass kneeling directly in front of her. That simple gesture touched me. Not wanting to miss a word of what Tao had to share, Sage humbly sat at her feet. It was how I felt from the moment I met Tao over two decades before and it made me instantly love and connect with Sage.

Tony smiled like a kid on Christmas morning. It was clear from the moment we all sat together that he had a love of learning and an enormous sense of respect for those older and wiser. The conversation unfolded in the most organic way. At the prompting of Tony's question, Tao shared what it was like to march with Gandhi at such a young age.

"It opened my eyes, you know? He was such a sweet and simple man. His power was in understanding people and wanting to help them. He wanted to help people learn to read and he told people if they wanted to help, that they should teach literacy in the villages because India WAS its villages. I learned how powerful peaceful actions could be. But you know this already. Look at your eyes. And your smiles. Both of you. Joanna told me the work you do in this world and it's very important."

Tony began to share about how many people his organization had helped feed in the past year. Watching this conversation was like watching spiritual soulmates on a first date. When people connect on a meaningful level, if you watch the light around them, it begins to glow. This ability to notice aura started for me when I first saw Tao's light brighten when she taught. It had since transferred to any moment where I witnessed true connection. Tao taught me that we were all able to see auras and light in this way, but that most, in their hurried pace of life, had stopped looking for it.

So many important and powerful topics followed. They discussed their shared beliefs about people, politics and religion. These are often subjects avoided in social situations. This was a true mastermind moment, a meeting of great minds interested in affecting true change. When Tao began to talk about the power of the mind and how she refuses to let anyone stop her from what she knew she was put here to do, Tony nodded his head vigorously in agreement. Sage told her that she saw her future-self in Tao and that she was sure Tony was seeing it too.

It was all beautiful. My visualization about this meeting had always been beautiful. The actualization of it was even better. I expected Tony and Sage to be curious about Tao in theory and in awe of her in reality. I had seen the impact she'd had on so many people for years. What I didn't expect, and what really touched me, was how generous of spirit they both were with me.

Tony fixed his attention on me. "So tell me, what's your story? How did you two meet?"

I shared about the first time I met Tao and the evolution of thought and feeling that I had experienced in the course of that one yoga class. I told him how I was hooked and that I wanted to learn anything and everything she could teach me.

"Smart. When life puts a mentor in your path, follow them. Their hindsight becomes your foresight. I had that with Jim Rohn."

"I know. I've followed your work for a long time and have always felt parallels with you and Tao. Maybe not in method but definitely in message."

"Having met her now I can see why," Tony replied.

"My intention for this lifetime is to be like an energetic lovechild of the two of you. I feel influenced and inspired by how you both help people to live their best lives. You're both focused on action and on acting NOW. I just didn't know the HOW. I didn't know how to make this meeting happen, so I focused on the what."

"How'd you do that, Joanna?"

Is Tony Robbins really this curious about my manifesting methods? I wondered. "I put a picture of the two of you on a vision board that I would see every day. Then I would visualize this meeting. In fact, I have seen this moment so often in my mind that its happening right now kind of makes this moment feel like a rerun."

"Right on."

Sage interjected, "So you've been with Tao ever since?"

"Yes. I'm sure you can feel her magic. I felt like I didn't know what I did to deserve having her in my life, but I certainly wasn't going to take for granted that I did."

Sage so kindly asked if we had gone to much trouble to meet with them. Tao told them all about baby River in the car with Mike. Tony asked a bunch of questions about how Mike and I met. I gave him the abridged story of returning from India where Tao said I would meet my maharaja only to find him in a strip club in New York City. He laughed heartily and inquired as to

Mike's line of work and all about our children. He kindly said that the next time we all got together, not to leave the Dude in the car and that we should all connect.

I glanced at Tao's face. The travel fatigue that I had witnessed only a few hours before after lunch was gone. Connection and conversation always energized her. A true extrovert, she loves people. This conversation was filling her up and I watched her and Sage holding hands and giggling. Their faces looked so pure and filled with light. I turned my gaze to Tony and noticed for the first time, the rainbow behind him. Magic begets magic. Look for it and you notice it everywhere.

After discussing saving the planet, stem cell technology, world hunger and the power of the breath, our chat was coming to an end. Tony and Sage so graciously offered to help promote anything Tao was doing, saying that her light and magic needed to be spread. They asked if we would be their guests at future events so that they could return the love we had shared. They asked if Tao would teach meditation and breathing to their students in the future. They took photos with her with the ocean behind them. Tao lifted a leg into tree pose as they smiled. I was recording every single detail in my mind and etching each moment into my heart.

When we first arrived, the assistant had mentioned that she thought Tony and Sage would have about a fifteen-minute window. Glancing at my watch, I realized we had been together for over an hour. We exchanged hugs and promises of further collaborations. While hugging Tony, I felt the pain in my now-hard breasts and realized that River must be missing me. Nursing was the best biological alarm system.

When we got back into the car with Mike, I exhaled. I sat in the backseat next to my River as Tao filled Mike in on all that had occurred. Tao was simply giddy.

"That was fun. I'd like to do more with them. You can tell they love what they do and do what they love. Isn't that important? They have a lovely home right on the water. You feel as if one step further and you'd be swimming. Yet, when you look into someone's eyes, you can see what they are about. He has the energy of a sweet little boy ready to change the world. And you know, that's what it takes to do it … childlike wonder and happy action. And his wife was wonderful, wasn't she? I really liked her. She was so beautiful but not just skin deep. She radiates, and when she holds your hand you feel her love."

I was reveling in this conversation. Tao's retelling of our experience made me so happy. I wanted so badly to make sure that she felt the value of our day trip to Florida. Taking a 99-year – old on a plane with a three-week-old baby was a bold move. I knew Tao said yes because she loved and trusted me. And then to hear her talk with Mike, I heard how genuinely excited she was, and that thrilled me beyond measure.

After returning the rental car at the airport, we went through security with Tao wowing each person she passed. The man who checked her passport could not get over the fact that she would soon be 100 and told everyone around us. Tao smiled as people continued approaching her all the way from security to our gate. Three people recognized her from different appearances and the rest were simply drawn to her. She gave advice, took selfies and hugged anyone who asked that of her. Even though I could tell she was beginning to feel the impact of the long day, she never missed a chance for connection. I nursed in the waiting area and at this point, the woman who had proclaimed to "know nothing about babies" was getting the routine. Tao lovingly helped me adjust the "Hooter Hider" that I used while nursing in public. She even offered to hold River and rock him if I was tired. As she held him, she touched the skin of his face and commented on how soft it was. The light that was streaming in from the large airport windows danced across Tao's face, and my eyes began to water as I took in that beautiful sight. One of my life's biggest miracles was holding another.

We settled into our seats for the short plane ride home. I wanted to let Tao sleep. Mike was holding River and I thought if I closed my eyes, perhaps that would encourage Tao to do so as well. But she had other ideas. After years of traveling with her, I had come to learn that some of my biggest moments of learning, or of personal growth, happened in the in between; on the way to, in breaks during, or coming home from our various events. This time was no exception.

"Thank you for always being so sweet with me."

"Are you serious, Tao? Thank YOU for being such a good sport. You let me kidnap you and take you to Florida simply because I told you I had a feeling it was meant to happen!"

"Well, I feel good when I'm with you. You have a light way of moving through the world and you embody what you teach. That is important. Too many people teach the things they don't live. You can feel the disconnect when that happens. With you, if you say it, I trust it's a good idea. I love the things we do together. And today was extra special. Your maharaja is the sweetest man. The two of you together have a dance. He takes care of you in a kind way. I see him look at you when you're not looking. And the way he holds the little baby is so gentle. What a sweet baby. He's so small and yet he sees the world better than most adults, really."

Whenever Tao was feeling chatty was my favorite time. With us tucked in the small airplane seats, my face turned toward hers, we were like young girls at a sleepover recapping the fun before finally falling asleep.

"Tao, today was beautiful for me. I've been so scared the past three weeks. When River was born, they took him away because he was having trouble breathing. He's been having a tough time getting enough milk and I just pray that he'll be able to gain weight. I've been so scared, and I haven't wanted to say it out loud because I didn't want to give my fears life. Today reminded me how powerful we all are at manifesting anything we want in this life."

Tao touched her cold hand to my flushed cheek. "Oh, Dear. That little boy is here for a reason. He's stronger and braver than you know. And YOU are stronger and braver than you know. Everyone is. You have learned the breath, you have practiced the breath, you have taught the breath. Any baby of yours will know the importance and the magic of this gift that is the breath. Don't let any doctor, or anyone else for that matter, put fear into your beautiful heart."

"Will River be okay?"

"Yes. He will be so much more than okay. I bet you he will be very smart. There is an intelligence in his eyes. And I already know that he will be a kind and gentle soul. Like Gandhi."

"You know what's funny, Tao? I thought he would be born on 10/3. I chose it because I love ones and threes ... like your birthday being on the 13th and my grandmother's on the 31st. But he came on 10/2, and I've been feeling like he had the wrong birthday; until yesterday. Someone told me that October 2nd was Gandhi's birthday."

"You see? He will be more than okay. He will change the world."

When Tao asked me to remind her of the name of the man whose house we'd just visited, I'd assumed she was tired enough that after I answered she'd give in to what must have been much needed rest. But she had other things in mind.

"I like what Tony and his wife are doing in this world. I would like to do more things with them."

"Okay, then we'll manifest that too. Tao, how do you feel?" The intimacy of the moment lent itself to me bravely asking what I usually didn't. "Are you still enjoying this lifetime?" The fatigue I had just noticed in her suddenly vanished. Her long response left me speechless.

"I do feel more tired than I used to, but I'm not done yet. There is so much left to do. I want to make it to 100 and have a party in India. I want to keep teaching and I want to keep dancing. There is so much I can do, but it isn't about me. I want to let people know that they each have a special magic. We can all change the world with kindness. If we want a peaceful world, we need peaceful individuals. So, every time someone does yoga, every time someone takes a good breath, every time someone meditates, they are feeling more peaceful. They are changing the world. Enough peaceful people will make for a peaceful world. That is what I want people to know. And why we need good teachers. Not just yoga teachers. We need parents, school teachers, friends, everyone to teach one another how to love, how to connect. We need the good people to have money and to use it to help our planet. We need to take care of our trees and our precious animals. We need to clean up our oceans. All of this is possible. I want to teach people to do what's on their mind and in their heart. That thought popped in there for a reason and we should not be afraid to follow our path or to do what is right. I have always told you, you will write a book. And I hope you write one for children. Because you are so great at working with the young ones, and the younger they are when they learn this practice of peace, the faster all of the other world changes will happen. I've been alive for a long time and I have lived through war. It's time for peace. It's time for love. And I want to see it."

Her words struck me so deeply that I hardly noticed the flight attendant brought Tao a steaming hot tea, just the way she liked it. I took her small and wrinkled hand in mine and watched her use the other one to take a sip of the tea. She placed it down on her tray and looked out the window.

Through the oval of glass, we watched the sun setting. We were flying above the clouds, with the sunset following us. Even more magical from this vantage point, I took in the explosion of colors. The reds, oranges, purples and magentas all on vivid display. Tao had also turned her gaze to take it all in before finally closing her sparkly-blue eyes.

EPILOGUE

Renee and I stood at the music console in the great hall at Kripalu. We spent the weekend with about 80 students who had flown in from all over the world to practice with Tao and celebrate her 100th birthday. It was incredible. Tao spread her light with her teachings, and her love with her connectedness. Each person lined up to take a photo with her before the final class began. We were due to head back home right after this session so Renee and I were tasked with making sure that it ended on time. Tao, not one to notice nor be governed by constructs such as time, would often go over.

Renee adjusted the lights and I lowered the music as this blessed woman brought the class into Savasana for their final meditation. All that was left were Tao's words:

> *Lie down on the ground in a perfectly balanced position, your feet slightly apart, arms outstretched, the palms facing upwards. Feel the space between the shoulders and buttocks, shut your eyes and try and let go of the outer world, your thoughts and the mental pictures which invade the mind.*
>
> *Tune into the lingering sun as with an explosion of colors, it brilliantly lights up the sky, then gently bids farewell as it sinks beyond the horizon.*
>
> *Surrender your whole being to the silence which seems to creep over the earth as dusk falls and listen suddenly to the rhythm of stillness. You can experience the vibrations of energy as you surrender deeper and deeper into the ground.*
>
> *Witness the belly and the pelvis rise and fall with your breath ... become the breath. The fire of creation of the solar plexus seems to glow like the setting sun. Your breath becomes deep, yet simple, like a cloud hanging in space. The mind now soft seems to merge within that space. Listen to the pulse beat of the earth, become one with your heart. Be the earth.*

Glide on the sound of your breath, like a seagull glides and seems to float over the ocean. Your breath seems to have wings as you become one with your inner self.

Allow the skin of your face and forehead to relax, relax the corners of your mouth, swallow. Soften the tongue as gently your breath is drawn through the subtle tissues of the body. Sense the broadness of your being as your entire body appears to melt into space. The waves of your breath seem to float into oneness with the eternal energy. And know that you are that energy.

Allow the muscles of the shoulders, neck and spinal column to melt into the stillness of universal peace, completely surrendering the physical body, letting go of your conscious mind. You seem to drift through space, through the door of life into the universal timeless power of the eternal. For you have opened the door of this internal power and feel the miracle within yourself as you witness the renewal of the body and mind, and relax.

Yogis believe that a new cycle begins every day as we become aware of this rejuvenation process.

Each rung of the ladder of life relates to the various chakras within the body. As you let go through this passage of timelessness, like the cycle of the sun and the moon, you are like the endless tides of the ocean, constantly flowing in and out, cleansing every cell in your body, every organ renewing. You become conscious that you have reached another dimension, one with this cosmic ocean wherein the power of the universe is deep and the silence never disturbed and the mind is brought to rest in the cradle of your heart.

ACKNOWLEDGMENTS

As my MOMMOM used to say when talking about our big, crazy family, "no one has what we have." Thank you for the roots to stay grounded and the wings to soar. Thank you for not getting me and yet still encouraging my dreams. Thank you to my mom, Bo, for being the nicest person, an endless source of love and support; and my dad, Atticus, for being the example of integrity and the voice in my head. Thank you to Aunt Judy for teaching me how to thank the academy when I was only six. My original siblings Jen and Jonny and all my bonus ones: my biggest laughs and favorite hugs; you're the reason I'm the weird one. Thank you to the nieces and nephews who have filled my heart and made me Aunt JoJo. And to LeeLee for expanding the family and baking the cookies. Our crew and our trips get better with each addition.

To the ancestry of teachers to whom Tao connected me and the legacy of students left in her wake, I am better for having you in my world.

Thank you to Bill for believing in *My Guru Wears Heels* and to Kenneth for refining it. And to Josh for so kindly putting up with my endless questions.

My Dude, the reality of you is even better than the dream. And the family and life we've created, an absolute fantasy. I love you. So so much.

River Vail, you made our family whole. Dream big our beautiful and kind miracle.

And to my two Taos ... may both the original and her namesake continue to be a beacon of light and an example of what's possible. Break every barrier ... and do it in heels.